*"Caricatures are often
the truest history of the times."*

Ralph Waldo Emerson

The American Presidency in Political Cartoons: 1776-1976

Thomas C. Blaisdell, Jr., Peter Selz and Seminar

Revised Edition

Peregrine Smith, Inc.

Salt Lake City and Santa Barbara

1976

Originally published by the University Art Museum,
Berkeley as a catalogue accompanying the exhibition
*The American Presidency in Political Cartoons: 1776-
1976*, January 13-February 22, 1976.

Schedule of the Exhibition

University Art Museum, Berkeley
January 13 / February 22, 1976

Lyndon Baines Johnson Presidential Library,
Austin, Texas
March 15 / April 25, 1976

The David and Alfred Smart Gallery,
University of Chicago
May 13 / June 27, 1976

Indianapolis Museum of Art
August 2 / September 12, 1976

National Portrait Gallery, Washington, D.C.
October 15 / November 28, 1976

President	Inauguration
George Washington	1789
John Adams	1797
Thomas Jefferson	1801
James Madison	1809
James Monroe	1817
John Q. Adams	1825
Andrew Jackson	1829
Martin Van Buren	1837
William H. Harrison	1841
John Tyler	1841
James K. Polk	1845
Zachary Taylor	1849
Millard Fillmore	1850
Franklin Pierce	1853
James Buchanan	1857
Abraham Lincoln	1861
Andrew Johnson	1865
Ulysses S. Grant	1869
Rutherford B. Hayes	1877
James A. Garfield	1881
Chester A. Arthur	1881
Grover Cleveland	1885
Benjamin Harrison	1889
Grover Cleveland	1893
William McKinley	1897
Theodore Roosevelt	1901
William H. Taft	1909
Woodrow Wilson	1913
Warren G. Harding	1921
Calvin Coolidge	1923
Herbert Hoover	1929
Franklin D. Roosevelt	1933
Harry S. Truman	1945
Dwight D. Eisenhower	1953
John F. Kennedy	1961
Lyndon B. Johnson	1963
Richard M. Nixon	1969
Gerald Ford	1974

The American Presidency in Political Cartoons: 1776-1976 is the work of a seminar co-sponsored by the Departments of History of Art and Political Science at the University of California, Berkeley. Under the direction of Professor Emeritus Thomas C. Blaisdell, Jr. and Professor Peter Selz, thirteen students spent a year's time studying the history of American political caricature, focusing on the office of the Presidency. Their efforts resulted in this publication, which accompanied an exhibition of the same name held at the University Art Museum, Berkeley in January/February 1976.

The original proposal for this project was made to the Museum by Professor Blaisdell. Professor Selz, who was then Director of the Museum, and the curatorial staff, immediately saw the immense potential which such an undertaking offered. Not only would the project provide an opportunity for the Museum to work with academic departments within the University, it would also be an appropriate and exciting celebration of the nation's bicentennial.

In their Acknowledgments, the authors have thanked those individuals and institutions whose generosity, assistance, and talents aided in the production of this book; I would like to add my thanks to theirs. To Professors Blaisdell and Selz and the members of the seminar we owe our admiration and appreciation. Their tremendous efforts made this publication a reality.

James Elliott
Director
June 1976

Acknowledgments

The American Presidency in Political Cartoons: 1776-1976 has been a cooperative venture. Students, faculty, staff and administrators of the University have taken part. They have been helped by generous contributions from several federal agencies, as well as from private institutions and individuals. Because this book grew out of an exhibition, it would be impossible not to acknowledge all those who have taken part in making this entire project a success.

The most important aspect of this book — the selection of the cartoons and the interpretations of them — were carried out by the thirteen students who took part in a seminar sponsored jointly by the Departments of the History of Art and Political Science. These students — Lani Abbott, Gretchen Beck, Judith Bernstein, Cheryl Brown, Danny Einstein, Ann Harlow, Linda Harris, Laura Kates, Gail Katz, Mark Manolson, Janet Potter, Mark Summers and Bradley Webb — spent much time in searching, studying and writing; their interest and hard work is evident in every aspect of this publication. (The initials of the students follow the essays on the cartoons.) Two other students, Zöe Baird and Joanne Jackson, were of great help in the origination of the project.

When the work of the seminar was completed, the staff of the University Art Museum, Berkeley, brought the exhibition and book to fruition. We wish to thank Curatorial Assistants Bonnie Earls and Nan Rosenbloom, in particular, for the many long hours they have spent on the exhibition and publication; Miss Earls in coordinating the abundance of loan information, and Miss Rosenbloom in editing and overseeing the production of the book. We also wish to thank Joy Feinberg, Curator of Collections and Exhibitions, for her overall curatorial coordination of the project; David Leonetti, Assistant Director/Administrative, for his handling of the financial matters relating to the exhibition and book; Bruce Montgomery, for his book design; Mya Pelletier, Registrar; and Carlos Gutierrez-Solana, Installations Coordinator. Former Acting Directors James Cahill and Jerrold Ballaine were supportive of the project, as was former Assistant Director/Curatorial, Brenda Richardson.

Within the University, several other individuals and organizations have been extremely gracious. Professor Norman Jacobson, Chairman of the Political Science Department, and Professor L. D. Ettlinger, former Chairman of the History of Art Department, made the seminar possible. Grateful acknowledgment is accorded to Chancellor Albert Bowker for the provision of funds to support the program. The Bicentennial Committee of the University, and its Chairman, Professor Garff Wilson, gave both moral and financial support to our project. The Committee for Arts and Lectures, particularly Professor Jerome Thomas, Vice-Chairman, and Ann Soengen, Secretary, was responsible for having cartoonist Herbert L. Block lecture at the University in conjunction with the exhibition. Dorothy Gregor and Joseph Rosenthal of The General Library made the University's collection of lithographs and engravings available to us. Various portions of the manuscript received editorial assistance from Nancy Becker, Ann Harlow and Lorna Price.

We are most appreciative of the generosity and cooperation of many agencies of the federal government. Those agencies which have custody of the cartoons — the Library of Congress and the Presidential Libraries —

were very kind in making them available for our exhibition. We wish to thank the following individuals for their particular help: Alan Fern, Director of the Prints Division of the Library of Congress, and his associates Morton Kaplan and Leonard Faber. The following Museum Curators were of great assistance: Gary A. Yarrington, of the Lyndon Baines Johnson Presidential Library; David Powers, of the John F. Kennedy Presidential Library; Will Jones, of the Dwight D. Eisenhower Presidential Library; James Whitehead, of the Franklin D. Roosevelt Presidential Library; Suzanne D. Rogers, of the Herbert Hoover Presidential Library; and Milton F. Perry, of the Harry S. Truman Presidential Library and Museum. James Rhoads, Archivist of the United States, and his associates John Jacobs and Daniel Reed, and John Spencer of the National Endowment for the Arts must also be thanked for their help and encouragement.

Robert Johnson, Curator in Charge, Achenbach Foundation for Graphic Arts, California Palace of the Legion of Honor, must be thanked for his gracious assistance with the various cataloguing problems the publication presented.

We are most grateful to the National Endowment for the Arts, Washington, D.C., for its financial support. Mrs. Harley C. Stevens must also receive our special thanks for her interest and generosity.

To the many lenders who have parted with their works, and to the living cartoonists who have been so gracious and generous, we owe our deepest appreciation.

We believe that all who have taken part in this book and exhibition have found great satisfaction and pleasure in this celebration of the Bicentennial.

Thomas C. Blaisdell, Jr.
Peter Selz

Preface

Peter Selz

In 1945, at the end of World War II, Pablo Picasso wrote in *Les Lettres Francaises* "...painting is not done to decorate apartments. It is an instrument of war for attack and defense against the enemy." This famous statement, made only a generation ago by the century's greatest artist, has all the more relevance at a time when so-called "color-field" painters under the guise of "modernism" decorate board rooms and the white, glazed expanses of banks with brightly painted acrylic stripes. Although most artists from Egyptian sculptors to today's "modernists" have been an arm of the Establishment, cartoonists and caricaturists have generally agreed with Picasso's pronouncement and have certainly been at their best when at their most critical. Caricature is an expressive, exaggerated, at times violent art. It cannot be analyzed in the formalistic language of such critics as Clive Bell, Roger Fry, or their present-day followers. "Significant Form" is rarely of concern to the man out to ridicule or destroy his political enemy; yet political art can achieve the intensities and heights of greatness to be found in the work of Hogarth, Goya, Daumier, George Grosz, John Heartfield, and Picasso.

There really is no such thing as abstract caricature, nor—to state the obvious—are the pictorial subjects of landscape or still life suitable for caricaturization, although of course, *paintings* of such subjects can be satirized, which, in a way is what Roy Lichtenstein has been doing with remarkable success, and perhaps this is what Eduard Manet did back in 1863 in his *Déjeuner sur l'herbe*. Caricature by its nature is descriptive and has its source in western art at the time of the Reformation and the Peasant Wars, when it was used as a very powerful weapon to deal with the hypocrisy of the Papacy, with suppression of the populace by feudal landlords, or when it attacked the then sacrilegious teachings of Luther and other reformers. From its very beginnings caricature is a literary and anecdotal art form. Whereas high art was brought to fruition under the patronage of church or princes, the flowering of caricature has its origins in popular art. We can learn a great deal more about the life of the people, their customs, their way of living, dress, and habits, from Holbein's woodcuts than from his paintings. But Holbein's woodcuts or Breughel's paintings and engravings are not caricature in the sense of *caricare*, i.e., to exaggerate. Even Leonardo's grotesque heads, which he called "physiognomic studies" were explorations of the frontiers of human form without the aspect of satire or comic purpose essential for the art form with which we are concerned here.

Caricature probably had its beginnings in the late 16th century in Bologna with the work of the Caracci who, precisely because they were engaged in idealizing the human form in the Grand Manner, rather than with attempting to copy nature, could also find enjoyment in exaggerating human features. It would seem that as long as artists were chiefly concerned with gaining a visual grasp on reality, the distortion of it was not yet possible. Caricature deals with truth—at least truth as seen by the caricaturist—which is different from beauty (*pace* Keats) as it is from reality. It often deals with ugliness and appears, therefore, precisely at the time when a norm of beauty is clearly established. Caricature is a form of wit or satire and as such usually has a moral purpose. It is not detached from life, and is more utilitarian than "pure art." Caricature is also bound by the time and place in which it was made and may, therefore, need more explication than pure painting or sculpture. While it can give us much information about the time, life, and thought of its origin, like other popular arts, it can date rather quickly. Yet, at its best, the political cartoon is able to retain amazing freshness and elicit an immediate response.

In their excellent essay on *Caricature*, the art historian E. H. Gombrich and the psychologist Ernst Kris suggest that the hidden and unconscious aim of fun, or wit, including caricature, is concerned with magic—that to copy a person, to mimic his behavior, is to annihilate his individuality. This is a shamanistic truth. The Navajos were aware of such dangers when they consistently prohibited artists or photographers from making visual records of their ceremonies, or any image of themselves. Perhaps because of this proscription they were able to maintain their culture when other Indian tribes had lost their identity. Today, when largely due to the abundance of media information and the semi-sophistication of the public, caricature—like most other forms of expression—has lost some of its direct power, it may be difficult to understand the seriousness with which this art form was approached in earlier times. Until the 17th century, artists were only permitted to draw the common people in a satirical fashion; only the humble could be seen as dogs or wolves or swine, whereas the exalted were not to be defaced.

Political caricature, or cartoon, as it began to be known in the 19th century, was feasible only after certain preconditions were established, primarily the general acceptance of a norm of beauty and the mental freedom to be able to separate the symbol (i.e., the drawing) from the reality of the person to be satirized, ridiculed or castigated.

In addition to these conditions, there also had to exist a climate of political freedom engendered by political stability, which permitted artists or writers to engage in satire. Such freedom first appeared in Europe in England under the Hanoverians at the end of the 17th century, and enabled writers like Daniel Defoe and Jonathan Swift to write their magnificent parables, and William Hogarth to eternalize the people—the rich and the wretched—of his time with moral passion and extraordinary artistic talent. He fused a classical sense of form with the popular tradition of Northern Europe, envisioning the world as a stage on which the human comedy is enacted.

Caricature is a graphic medium and for that reason required further preconditions to its development: the invention of mass printing methods and the availability of a support, i.e. paper, on which the image could be imprinted. In order for caricature to be effective, furthermore, a system for its distribution had to exist; over the centuries this system changed from broadsheets to humor magazines, and finally to newspapers.

The vocabulary of printmaking reflects a clear comprehension of the artist's attitude which, especially in printed caricature, is one of attack. The printmaker working in a wooden block would *cut* into it, while the etcher uses a *needle* as well as *acid* to create the desired *bite*. Rare indeed is a good political cartoon in which the artist tries to show his subject in a favorable light.

Although a few early American cartoons were woodcuts, and there are occasional etchings, the majority were engravings issued as broadsheets. Engraving had been the medium of Hogarth, and of his important successors Thomas Rowlandson, George Cruikshank, and James Gillray. Gillray was actually the first artist to specialize in political cartoons, whether commentaries on the social scene in England, biting attacks on the French Revolution or an occasional charge against these new United States. The earliest American political prints come, interestingly enough, from the hands of illustrious political leaders, such as Benjamin Franklin's "Join or Die" of 1754 which appeared in many newspapers from Philadelphia to Boston, or Paul Revere's color engraving, "The Boston Massacre" of 1770, anti-British propaganda under the guise of a realistic rendering of the event. Franklin was a printer by trade and Revere not only a silversmith but also an engraver.

Since the printmaker is intimately involved with the tools and techniques at his command, the medium has always had an important effect on his work. In engraving, the artist works slowly with a cutting tool, the burin. The engraved plate is inked and thereafter wiped clean until the ink remains only in the engraved lines. The prepared plate, overlaid with a sheet of dampened paper, is passed through a press, the pressure of which forces the paper fibers into contact with the ink-filled recessed lines of the plate. Fine details can be successfully reproduced by this technique. Most political cartoons of the early years of the United States were printed in this manner, but actually, since newsprint for broadsheets or even for newspaper was very scarce, few political cartoons exist, especially in the period before Andrew Jackson was elected President in 1828. Stylistically the early cartoons follow British examples to a considerable extent, as in the work of William Charles, himself a Scot. Originality was not an issue of great importance at the time. As a matter of fact, it can be observed in general that the political cartoonist is not so much concerned with originality of form or content as is the painter or sculptor, much as a similar observation can be made about

journalism when compared with poetry or prose. In contrast to English models, American cartoons, often cluttered with people with speech balloons issuing from their mouths, were simpler and more primitive in style. There was no Royal Academy propagating the Grand Manner in the United States. In early American cartoons, there is more humor in the verbal messages than in the caricaturist's distortions or the quality of their drawing.

In 1796, Alois Senefelder of Bavaria discovered a new technique which subsequently transformed printmaking. Lithography is a swift and inexpensive printing method based on the principle that oil and water do not mix. The artist draws his image with wax crayon on a smoothly dressed granite stone. The image is fixed chemically in the stone and the stone itself is moistened with water, then inked. The crayon image repels water but attracts and holds ink whereas the crayoned wet areas of stone repel the ink. Stone and overlaid paper are passed through the litho press to obtain a mirror-reversed image, as in all printing. Great subtlety of shading can be achieved in lithography, and the production of colored lithographs is easily accomplished by using a series of stones, one stone for each color to be added to the finished image.

Lithography made printmaking easy and, most important, rapid. The technique of drawing directly on stone encouraged a loose style appropriate to art for popular media. The artist could make his drawing, then leave the rest of the labor to the printer. The lithographer stone's surface, unlike the engraved plate, does not break down after repeated use. Lithograph images may be pulled indefinitely, in almost unlimited numbers. The ease of preparing a stone and of drawing on it—unlike the laborious, time-consuming preparation of an engraving plate—made lithography an ideal technique to distribute popular art forms, to edit political material whose timeliness might be crucial to the effectiveness of its message, and to serve the demands of an ever-widening public.

Lithography became popular almost at once. It reached its zenith in France in the work of Honoré Daumier, who made some 4,000 lithographs for the humor magazines *Caricature* and *La Charivari*, both initiated in Paris in the 1830s. Here Daumier made caricature into a monumental statement. His observations of man, his artistic invention and brilliant draftmanship, his deep sense of human dignity and outrage at repression, have never been equalled.

While the profound humanism and political acuity of Daumier was not attained by artists in the United States, American caricaturists began to flourish in the Jacksonian era. Andrew Jackson himself, the first American "log cabin" President, broke with the Federalist tradition whereby only members of the intellectual and social elite were elected to the highest office. Jackson was a man of colorful personality who provoked the kind of controversy necessary to produce good cartoon images. Lithography, introduced just before his election, enabled the art of cartooning to spread, especially after large printing houses such as Currier and Ives began to produce vast quantities of prints. Most cartoons of the pre-Civil War period, however, were rather hackneyed—predictable and naive both in drawing and political awareness. No powerful social satirist, no individual of personal vision comparable to Hogarth or Daumier, emerged on these shores. It must furthermore be kept in mind that Andrew Jackson's personal magnetism notwithstanding, Congress, rather than the President, was of prime interest to the public. Jackson's suc-

cessors moreover, were men of no particularly strong individuality or power. In fact, this country was served by a series of mediocre Presidents, uninteresting individuals who did not call forth the kind of energy necessary to inspire work of very high quality by cartoonists.

Even when Abraham Lincoln, a President whose personality was in every way fascinating, came to the White House in 1861, he was generally accorded pejorative treatment by cartoonists. Particularly during his first term, he was often portrayed by them as foolish and incompetent, an image encouraged by Lincoln's gawky, countryman appearance, his high-pitched nasal Illinois twang, and his lewd barnyard humor. But as Lincoln gained extraordinary powers during the Civil War and extended the reach of his office to unprecedented levels of authority, cartoonists such as Frank Bellew began to realize that here was a President whose historic significance was evident, and whose intellectual stature, despite his mannerisms, was unique. Lincoln's bony frame, his craggy face, and inimitable bearing came to dominate cartoon images of him.

In England, where political opinion favored the Confederacy, Lincoln was sharply attacked by Sir John Tenniel, famous for his illustrations of Lewis Carroll's *Alice in Wonderland*. Matt Morgan, who later came to the United States, also made Lincoln his target. No American cartoonist had the skill or bite of Tenniel or Morgan. In fact, most of the important American cartoonists throughout the 19th century were foreign-born and largely foreign-trained. William Charles had come from Scotland. Bellew, the most original cartoonist at mid-century, was born in India of British parents. Frank Leslie, who was to publish the first successful humor magazine in America, was also born in England, as were William Newman and Matt Morgan, who did fine cartoons for Leslie's *Weekly*. Dr. Adalbert Volck, a practicing dentist in Baltimore, who did fine anti-Union cartoons in secret, came from Germany, as did America's greatest cartoonist, Thomas Nast. In the next generation, the leading men in the field were also foreign born: Joseph Keppler came from Austria and Bernard Gillam from England. Perhaps a chief reason explaining the lack of an important native American cartoonist during the 19th century was the fact that no formal standards of visual beauty had been established here, and therefore there were no clear norms to distort. Fidelity to nature was by-and-large the aim of serious art in America.

At mid-century, humor magazines flourished not only in Paris, but also in London where, in 1841, *Punch* was first published. Germany had its *Fliegende Blätter*, and *Kladeradatsch*, Austria its *Kikeriki*. Similar attempts in the United States met at first only with the briefest success, largely because they lacked a true sense of satire and humor, as one observer of the time remarked: "Many funerals are conducted in a manner far better calculated to minister to the sense of the ridiculous."[1] It was only when Frank Leslie established his *Illustrated Weekly* in 1855, to be followed by *Harper's Weekly* two years later, that humor magazines became successful in this country, a success owed largely to the extraordinary talent of one artist, Thomas Nast.

Nast, who began working for *Leslie's Illustrated Newspapers* (its original name), in 1855 at the age of fifteen, became America's first major political cartoonist. The German-born Nast had come to New York at the age of six. In 1860 he sailed for England and soon thereafter he joined Garibaldi's revolutionary forces in Italy as a correspondent. It seems quite likely that this experience also helped shape his own strong political stance. In 1862, again in America, he was hired by *Harper's Weekly* to send back sketches from the battlefields of the Civil War. These sketches were as significant in the history of American political cartoons as were Matthew Brady's photographs for the history of photography.

Having no major American standards, Nast chose English cartoonists, men like James Gillray, John Leech, and especially Sir John Tenniel as his models. During his stay in Europe he also managed to study in the museums of Italy, France, Germany, and England, and somehow learned enough history and literature to fill his work with allusions to classical literature, Shakespeare, Cervantes, and the *Arabian Nights*.

Interestingly enough, Thomas Nast preferred the laborious process of wood engraving to the ease of lithography. Wood engraving creates a relief; the artist, working on an end-grain block, cuts away with knife or gouge all areas of the surface not intended to print. Wood engraving was developed to a high state of competence by Thomas Bewick in London in the late 18th century, and is a technique by means of which a great variety of shades and precise fine lines can be achieved, qualities unique to this process.

Thomas Nast's reputation as a great cartoonist is based solidly on his 1871 drawings attacking Boss Tweed and the Tammany Ring, prompting Tweed's famous demand to "stop them damn pictures." But Nast persisted in his campaign with biting eloquence until this particular crook, who had corrupted the entire city government of New York, was ousted from office. Boss Tweed escaped to Spain, was recognized there from one of Nast's cartoons published in *Harper's Weekly*, extradited to the United

States and ended his days in a New York jail. A clear example of the effect of art on politics!

Nast was active and highly effective in every Presidential campaign for over two decades, supporting Republicans until the nomination of Grover Cleveland in 1884. Ulysses S. Grant stated that Nast's pencil helped him win his office. In his editorial cartoons Nast formalized the basic iconography of the American political cartoon with such symbols as the Democratic Donkey and—his own inventions—the Republican Elephant and the Tammany Tiger and stamped these symbols on the American mind. When he left *Harper's Weekly* in 1887, his departure was partly responsible for the decline of that journal. He, in turn, lost his chief stage and political power. There was also the question of technological obsolescence: as photomechanical processes of reproduction were increasingly used in magazines and newspapers toward the end of the century, Nast's wood-engraving style went out of fashion and artists skilled in the new technique became popular.

"The great events in the nineteenth century history of prints were the discoveries of photography and the attendant photo-mechanical processes."[2] William Ivins goes on to assert that "in the whole history of human communication it is doubtful if any more extraordinary step had ever been taken than this."[3] The invention of photography, of course, pre-empted many of the informational and reportorial purposes of the older print techniques. But the use of photochemical processes for half-tone reproductions of both black and white and color prints made a new and cheaper way of visual communication practical.

By these means it became cheaper to produce cartoons, and during the last quarter of the 19th century, as America expanded economically and grew more prosperous, people could begin to relax, enjoy life and laugh at themselves. Large new humor magazines were founded, such as Joseph Keppler's *Puck*. Keppler, a Viennese actor and artist, had come to St. Louis in 1867 and established *Die Vehme* and then *Puck*—both in German. He then went to New York and by 1877 he brought out an English edition of *Puck* which became highly successful because of his elaborate colored cartoons of trenchant satire and light-hearted wit, which appeared on the front and back covers as well as the centerfold of the weekly. Like Nast, Keppler did not resort to speech balloons and banderoles; he also used many Shakespearean and other literary references in his captions. His important competitor was the English-born cartoonist Bernard Gillam, whose sparkling work graced the pages of *Judge*, founded in 1881. (Another humor magazine, *Life*, appeared at this time; it was, however, more interested in social satire than in political commentary.) *Puck* and *Judge* exerted enormous political influence at the end of the century, primarily because of their large editorial political cartoons. Although they continued to exist until World War I, it was the daily newspaper that began to provide the chief platform for cartoonists at the turn of the century.

The newspaper cartoons which began to proliferate during the early years of the 20th century are simpler in style and freer in execution. When daily deadlines had to be met, there simply was not the time for the careful elaboration of the color lithographs of the humor magazines. Cartoonists now worked largely in pen and ink and their drawings were reproduced photomechanically by the daily presses. Newspapers all over the country from New York to San Francisco, eventually employed their own home cartoonists.

William Randolph Hearst managed to attract two particularly able individuals to his *New York Journal*. One of them, Frederick Burr Opper, had worked for *Puck* for some eighteen years and had developed a style of whimsical and droll drawings, filled with funny Lilliputian creatures. His work was similar to the drawings Lyonel Feininger was doing in Berlin for German humor magazines, as well as for the *Chicago Tribune*. Opper's mischievous comic strip wit was in contrast to the work of Homer Davenport, whom Hearst brought from New York for the *San Francisco Examiner*. Davenport had a visual imagination and power which had not been seen since the days of Thomas Nast. One of his memorable works, a cartoon done in 1900 for the front page of the *Journal*, depicts the figure of the Cleveland capitalist Mark Hanna —gross, fat, his suit covered with dollar signs and labor's skeleton beneath his feet— standing on the pedestal from which he has usurped George Washington, whose statue in front of the U.S. Treasury Building on Wall Street is being carted away to make room for Hanna, the true political power in his day. Other cartoonists who began to make important contributions to the political life of the early part of the century were men such as T. McCutcheon, who had started with the *New York Evening Post* and then worked for the *Chicago Daily Tribune* for 43 years; Clifford K. Berryman of the *Washington Star* and Jay N. Darling ("Ding"), who drew about 17,000 rather intricate cartoons with a conservative message for the *Des Moines Register* and the *New York Tribune*.

Newspaper cartoonists, as well as the men who continued working for the humor magazines, were lucky in having a fabulous subject in the White House for two terms. Theodore Roosevelt was a controversial, ruthless man of great energy and physical prowess. His appearance, with his toothy broad grin, his thick glasses and his walrus mustache, were perfect grist for the cartoonist's mill. Even better, of course, were the behavior and the verbal expressions of the carrier of the Big Stick, the self-styled Trust-Buster, the Rough Rider, the Gunboat Diplomat, the Muckracker, the Bull Moose, the Big Game Hunter, Teddy.

The style of political cartooning changed little during the next decades. Cartoonists amused themselves with the enormous bulk of William Howard Taft or ridiculed the scholarly personality, the progressive stance and reforming zeal of Woodrow Wilson, who by cartoonists like Iowa's "Ding" and others was frequently shown as a woman— which was bad enough—but worst of all as a schoolmarm. Nothing really, could have been more degrading for an American President. Who, in these United States would want a scholar or a teacher for the highest office in the land? The anti-intellectualism which had its beginnings in American political life with Andrew Jackson had become all-pervasive and was reflected in the work of the cartoonists who were, after all, in the employ of the newspapers. During World War I most cartoonists actively engaged in patriotic propaganda for recruiting or selling Liberty Bonds, as did the many artists who produced the flood of war posters of the time.

A very different kind of cartooning was to be seen in the Socialist magazine, *The Masses*, founded by Max Eastman in 1911. With John Sloan as art editor many of America's leading painters and draftsmen, among them George Bellows, Robert Minor, Boardman Robinson, Stuart Davis and Art Young, contributed to this left-wing journal. However, most of these artists were not really cartoonists and were willing to work as illustrators for the sake of their political beliefs. Rarely indeed did *The Masses* or its successors, *The Liberator*, *The Worker's Monthly*, and *The New Masses* publish cartoons against a President, because as Marxist journals, they were more concerned with fighting the system than with taking issue with any individual. Art Young, Sloan's successor as art editor of *The Masses* and a man able to combine a great sense of satire with a powerfully drawn line, produced a series of superb cartoons, explaining that "practically all of them are generalizations on the one important issue of this era the world over: Plutocracy versus the principles of Socialism...."[4] While these men may not have created prints of the political and artistic incisiveness and perspicacity of a George Grosz or an Otto Dix, they certainly developed a socially conscious art, which recorded the miserable condition of the American working class, in opposition to the newspaper establishment, which ignored it.

Their serious satire was only rarely picked up by the world of official cartooning, although an excellent artist like Daniel R. Fitzpatrick of the *St. Louis Post-Dispatch* was clearly influenced by his more radical colleagues. During the post-war period, cartooning became an increasingly accepted field of journalism and the Pulitzer Prize Committee established a special award category for cartooning, the award to be determined, interestingly enough, by a jury of journalists rather than artists or art critics. Rollin Kirby, a good draftsman distinguished by his free and sketchy line who was working for the *New York World*, received the first Pulitzer Prize for a political cartoon in 1922 and was honored by two additional Pulitzer Prizes in the years to follow. It was Kirby who invented the humorous figure of Mr. Dry, a ragged bum with umbrella and silk hat who showed a slight resemblance to Daumier's Ratapoil. After Prohibition (a highly popular topic

for the cartoonist) became a dead issue, there were the more serious matters of the Depression, Fascism and World War II to deal with, as well as that most colorful personality, Franklin Delano Roosevelt.

The second Roosevelt had a splendid, large-jowled face, a long cigarette holder, a broad grin, a mysterious smile. His strong stands on a variety of economic and political issues—generally very controversial ones—made this four-term President and world leader a great subject for satire of all kinds on the part of American and foreign cartoonists, noteworthy among which were the clever and delightful Art Déco drawings of Mexico's Miguel Covarrubias for *Vanity Fair* and the caricatures of England's David Low, whose brilliant wit, broad and forceful line, and political insight made him the finest caricaturist of his time. *The New Yorker*, founded in 1925, became the leading organ for cartoons in America after the older humor magazines folded. It established its own sophisticated style of drawing, particularly appealing to both the intellectual and social elite. It managed to attract such outstanding talent as Peter Arno, James Thurber and the inimitable Saul Steinberg—men, however, whose wit in general was not directed toward the President.

During the post-war years editorial newspaper cartoons—like other forms of journalism—increasingly became syndicated, so that the same cartoon, be it Harry Truman's frozen smile, Eisenhower playing golf with his office, or John F. Kennedy as the charismatic Knight of Camelot, could be chuckled over at the breakfast table from Boston to Los Angeles. New cartoonists reached great popularity in the post-war years, men such as Bill Mauldin who had first come to national attention with his satirical drawings for *Stars and Stripes*, in which he showed the true foxhole experiences of "Willie and

Joe." In the *St. Louis Post-Dispatch* and later the *Chicago Sun-Times*, Mauldin continued his ironic attacks on the establishment, being a particularly strong advocate of civil rights. Herbert L. Block (Herblock), working for the *Washington Post*, established his own influential style—partially indebted to the American comic strip—a style which relies as much on the salty wit of his verbal as on his visual message. He became the most admired political cartoonist of a generation, especially after he carried out a powerful campaign against Joe McCarthy's witchhunts and associated hysterical anti-Communist activities of the 1950s. Although he did not measure up to Thomas Nast as an artist, Herblock once more became a political force so that Richard M. Nixon, who has always been a favorite subject of liberal cartoonists, said in 1960, upon receiving the Republican nomination for the Presidency: "I have to erase the Herblock image."[5]

Cartoonists had a field day with Lyndon Baines Johnson, with his big Stetson hat and his friendly Texan drawl about the "Great Society," and his long justification of a debilitating war in Southeast Asia that many still consider to have been illegal. Indeed, Johnson's schizophrenic politics and Nixon's unmitigated lust for absolute power, by means of which criminals were able to masquerade as apostles of "law and order," created an Orwellian situation which renewed the force of political cartooning. It was, in fact, the resulting disillusionment with politics on the part of the young that brought new life to the American political cartoon, originating largely in the underground press, the political poster, and other manifestations of counter-culture. The more orthodox political cartoonists, Herblock and Mauldin, Pat Oliphant, Paul Conrad, Hugh Haynie and Lou Grant were followed by a new crop of draftsmen, men such as Robert Grossman,

David Levine, Ranan Lurie, Robert Pryor, Edward Sorel and Paul Szep. These cartoonists, unlike their predecessors, went to art schools such as the Ontario College of Art, the Art School of Cooper Union, or Pratt Institute. Levine even went to Hans Hofmann's art school in New York, although little of the abstractionist's push-pull theory of painting is evident in the art of the young draftsman.

Today, as in the 19th century, many of the younger American cartoonists are foreign born and trained. Pat Oliphant, syndicated from the *Los Angeles Times* is Australian, and his intricate, droll, and often involuted style is indebted to England's famous social cartoonist, Ronald Searle. Canadian born Paul Szep, called the "Boston Strangler" on account of his virulent attacks on corruption and hypocrisy, developed a highly individualistic drawing style. Ranan Lurie, who was born in Israel and studied there, as well as in Paris, is a professional painter as well as a cartoonist; his work appears in New York, London, Paris, and Israel. All of these men, as well as Edward Sorel (whose book, *Making the World Safe for Hypocrisy*, is a superb example of the new art of satire) and Harold M. Talburt, have brought new vitality to the political cartoon in America.

Another source for the new art of political satire is the renewed popularity and sophistication of the comic strip. Jules Feiffer, a playwright and filmmaker as well as cartoonist who draws a strip cartoon for the *Village Voice* and *Playboy* was largely responsible for bringing politics back into the world of the comic strip. His example has recently been followed by Garry Trudeau's highly popular "Doonesbury."

The renaissance of the political cartoon in America was certainly unpredictable. It seemed, for a time, that the purpose and function of the political cartoon was a matter of the past. For one thing, a valid form of beauty from which the cartoonist could diverge no longer exists in the visual arts. Once distortion became completely accepted as art, whether the personal emotional impulse of the Expressionists, the surgical breakdown of the human form into geometric planes by the Cubists, or the transformation of the human figure into fantastic dream images by the Surrealists, it became very difficult for the cartoonist to find his own form of distortion. Cartoonists, therefore, went on, doing their editorial jobs at a remove from the developments in high art. Things became even more difficult, however, when an artist like Roy Lichtenstein became extolled by critics, art galleries, and museums for his painted lampoons of cartoons and comic strips. What, now, remained for the professional cartoonist himself to do?

Another problem facing the cartoonist during these last twenty years has been the competition of the visual media. How may he possibly rival the reality of seeing the actual horror of Mai Lai on the evening news, or with witnessing the faces of our political leaders during the Congressional hearing by the McCarthy or the Ervin Committees?

But art and the history of art remains unpredictable. Political art which, in America, had become pretty much extinct after the late 1930s and the disillusionment of radical artists with the Hitler-Stalin pact, became a new reality in the 1960s. Cartoonists again engaged themselves in the battle against war and corruption. They grew a great deal more aggressive, when America was engaged in aggression in Viet Nam, and even more so when the administration attempted all kinds of tricks—old and new—to stifle the free press. Suddenly—and this is a very recent development—art galleries which heretofore had used their space only for high art, began showing drawings by political cartoonists. The very concept of art began to expand. During the last decade, art has increasingly become a part of life rather than the special concern of artist and cognoscenti. In the last ten years, artists have created earthworks in the desert, curtains across canyons, protest murals in the ghettos. Happenings, environments, street art, body art, process art, conceptual art, all have expanded the range of art far beyond what had been known or accepted before. With Viet Nam and Watergate, political protest art has once again found a wide following in America, a source of strength for the battle against the Establishment. Brilliant caricaturists, above all David Levine working in the *New York Review of Books*, renewed the art of the political caricature with his whimsical, old-fashioned style of shaded drawing, resulting in works of trenchant, devastating, sardonic wit. Levine's politicians generally carry their own attributes, be they Churchill's cigars, LBJ's stomach scar in the shape of the map of Viet Nam, Nixon eating grapes while embracing a swine. A great caricaturist, Levine expresses his passionate protest by means of poignant satire with a result that affects the attitudes of the viewer. Even President Ford, gazing forlornly at a gallery of U.S. political cartoons, recently conceded, "The pen is mightier than the politician."[6]

Notes
1. Richard Grant White, "Caricature and Caricaturists," *Harper's New Monthly Magazine*, April, 1862, p. 606.
2. William M. Ivins, Jr., *Prints and Visual Communication*, Cambridge, Mass., 1953, p. 115.
3. *Ibid.*, p. 177.
4. Stephen Hess and Milton Kaplan, *The Ungentlemanly Art*, New York, 1966, p. 143.
5. John D. Weaver, "Drawing Blood," *Holiday*, August, 1965, p. 72.
6. Stanley Kanfer, "Editorial Cartoons: Capturing the Essence," *Time*, Feb. 3, 1975, p. 63.

The Changing Presidency

Thomas C. Blaisdell, Jr.

The Presidency was created by the Constitution in a different sense than the Congress and the Supreme Court which were continuations of preexisting governmental forms. The Congress grew out of British parliamentary practice, refined and purified in many ways by colonial assemblies, pre-revolutionary conventions and conferences, "state" governments and by the Articles of Confederation. The Constitutional Convention itself was a form of "congress." The Court, too, had a long history in the principles and procedures of the courts of the United Kingdom and the colonies and in the principles of common law. The Presidency was different for it was a new office.

The President was not intended to be a king. Sovereignty did not rest with him, but with the people. His oath of office was to "preserve, protect and defend the Constitution of the United States." The Constitution, however, created a tri-partite government which left a great deal of ambiguity as to what the President's oath to support the Constitution meant.

One of the immediate problems facing the new government was establishing the working relations between the Presidency, the Congress and the Supreme Court. Theoretically, the Congress makes laws and levies taxes and the President provides for their execution. Similarly, in theory, the Courts make decisions and the President carries them out. In practice, however, the Congress often administers its own laws, as in the so-called "independent agencies" of government, and Congressional committees often closely supervise government departments, as in the case of the Joint Committee on Atomic Energy. Likewise, the Courts may administer laws with greater rigor than

the executive branch would choose. In using its authority to determine the Constitutionality of laws, the Court is often accused of "legislating." These categories of legislating, executing and judicating are not clear and simple. Much of the history of the Presidency rests on the way in which Presidents have interpreted this power to "execute."

We will examine two major features of the office of the Presidency. The first of these is the significant fluctuation in the power of the office as it has been administered by successive Presidents. The second characteristic is the relationship of the Presidency to the other two branches of government. When a President is strong Congress tends to be less effective and often gives the President powers which he finds difficult to use. On the other hand, when the Congress or the Court has strong leadership, either can make the Presidency seem secondary.

The basis of the President's powers are set down in the Constitution. The President is the chief executive of the federal government, and has limited veto powers over legislation, consultative powers with the Senate over the appointment of judges, ambassadors, civil and military officials, and powers of commander-in-chief of the armed forces during times of war. To see how these powers of the Presidency have developed over the years, the following brief sections will examine the use of these powers by the men who have held the office:

I. Washington to John Quincy Adams
II. Jackson to Buchanan
III. Lincoln and Johnson
IV. Grant to McKinley
V. Theodore Roosevelt to Hoover
VI. Franklin D. Roosevelt to Ford

The purpose of the Constitution was to form "a more perfect union." The earliest leaders of the new nation-state were largely the men who had written the Constitution, among whom one of the most important was President George Washington. He had not only led the armies and been a leader of those working for independence, but he had also presided over the Constitutional Convention. While many had contributed to the drafting of the Constitution, it was Washington's firm hand that made the final document possible.

All of the early Presidents realized that it was necessary for the President to be recognized as head of state. Washington took steps to demonstrate that he was President by participating in an imposing inauguration ceremony, by traveling widely to allow himself to be seen, and by insisting that Governors should call upon him first — rather than the reverse.

While he regarded these symbolic displays of power as important, he was equally as ready to use his powers as commander-in-chief to establish the reality of this authority. In the flareup known as the Whiskey Rebellion, distillers had refused to pay excises levied on the whiskey they were making. They changed their minds quickly when faced with the military strength of the new government. Washington also used his position as commander-in-chief in conjunction with his powers to negotiate treaties and advise Congress, when he issued a proclamation of this country's neutrality in relationship to the ongoing European wars.

While Washington's use of his powers as commander-in-chief was important, his major task was to organize the executive branch. This involved appointing personnel and determining their responsibilities. Washington's small cabinet consisted of a Secretary of State, to handle official domestic as well as foreign affairs, a Secretary of the Treasury, to collect taxes and to control expenditures, and a Secretary of War, to be responsible for military affairs. These positions were complemented by an Attorney General and a Postmaster General. All of these men were heads of their departments and personal advisors to the President; they were in no sense a collective cabinet responsible to Congress as was the British custom.

Alexander Hamilton, who was appointed as the country's first Secretary of the Treasury, was a driving executive who regarded himself as responsible to Congress, as well as to the President. He established such good rapport with Congress that, for many years after, Presidents were handicapped by the Treasury being regarded as having a unique relationship to Congress. Hamilton was also instrumental in having the First Bank of the United States established. This action created a precedent for separating major monetary and financial functions from the Presidency, an issue around which struggles have continued until today.

There was no question of the President's authority to make personnel appointments. However, since these were made with the "advice and consent" of the Senate, the question was promptly raised as to whether the President could dismiss any appointee without the consent of the Senate. The issue was decided by the tie-breaking vote of Vice-President Adams presiding in the Senate. It was one of the most important acts of a Vice-President, but the issue was to arise again in later years.

One of President Washington's final acts, his decision not to be a candidate for a third term, established a custom which was not broken until President Franklin D. Roosevelt. Later, the Twenty-second Amendment legally limited the President to two terms. Many students of the Presidency, who believe that customs can be more useful than laws, have questioned the wisdom of this amendment.

President Adams agreed with Washington's interpretation of a strong Presidency. He accepted the Federalist position which gave great importance to federal and Presidential status and, in accord with this interpretation, Congress passed the Alien and Sedition Acts. This legislation declared it a crime to "defame" the President, the Congress or the federal government, and many Republicans (Jefferson's party) were jailed and fined. Kentucky and Virginia declared the laws void in their states. Adams attempted to maintain a neutral stance towards both England and France during the Napoleanic period. Fortunately he succeeded, but in the process he divided his Federalist support and lost his reelection to Jefferson.

Jefferson was a master of Congressional relations, but his greatest success was in his use of Presidential authority. In negotiating the Louisiana Purchase, he overstepped his Constitutional authority, an action which he justified on grounds of overwhelming desirability and necessity and which was accepted by Congress. Jefferson also succeeded in persuading Congress to pass the Embargo Acts, which were an attempt to pressure England and France to stop interfering with American shipping. Even though this legislation was administered with great skill, it divided the country and had to be modified.

When Jefferson was succeeded by Madison, the problem of restrictions on foreign trade again caused conflicts. The Congress was teeming with young western representatives who were unwilling to limit the country to economic warfare: they forced Madison to declare the War of 1812. The President had little military or economic support to carry on a war. The eastern seaboard was open to attack from the British fleet and there were major defeats. The United States also suffered defeats on the Canadian frontier. There were some naval successes on the Great Lakes and, in the struggle for the Mississippi Valley, General Andrew Jackson finally led his troups to a major victory. However, this victory had no influence on the peace treaty which had been signed before this battle took place; a treaty which dealt with none of the issues at stake. Nevertheless, ironically, the war was looked upon as a great success on the grounds that American soldiers had fought bravely against the experienced British forces.

Monroe's Presidency, too, called for Presidential leadership in foreign affairs. Using troops of the war which had just ended, General Jackson was sent to Florida, which was still occupied by Spain, and where settlers were complaining of Indian harassment. Following the defeat of the Indians and the occupation of the Spanish capitol, Pensacola, Spain found it necessary to sell Florida to the United States. Monroe also used his authority to send naval forces against Tripoli, Algiers and Tunis to stop interference with American shipping and to stop claims for tribute.

Best known of Monroe's foreign policy actions is probably the Monroe Doctrine, which stated that European attempts to establish new colonies on the American continent would be regarded as "dangerous to our peace and safety." John Quincy Adams, who, as Secretary of State, had been most influential in persuading Monroe to take this action, was to succeed Monroe as President. Adams was the last of the Presidents who were, in effect, the products of the Congressional caucus. New forces broadened the electorate and shifted the power to nominate to party conventions. Andrew Jackson, who became President under the new system, marks the beginning of another phase in the struggle for power between the President and Congress.

JACKSON TO BUCHANAN

The issues around which the powers of the President centered during the second quarter of the 19th century were western and southern expansion (which often meant displacing Indians), monetary and banking policy, and wide use of the appointing power which was used to build party strength in local machines as well as to perform government services. All of these issues were overshadowed, however, by the growing significance of slavery. In the South it was inherent in the plantation system. In the North there was fear of competition between black and white labor. Over all was the moral problem of human rights. Jackson demonstrated Presidential power and leadership in all these fields, but the next three administrations were dominated by Congress. It might have been expected that one of the strong men of the Congress would have been nominated for the Presidency, but in the nominating conventions these men tended to block each other and weak men were chosen as nominees. The Presidencies of Van Buren, Harrison and Tyler gave no strong leadership; it was not until the Presidency of Polk that we again find an example of a strong President.

Jackson was a domineering personality who exercised strong Presidential power. His principal actions in international affairs had to do with Indian affairs which were,

Constitutionally, affairs of the federal government. Jackson ordered the Indians to move so that their land could be expropriated by the federal government. The process by which this was done was a combination of asserting authority and claiming lack of authority. Historically, Jackson had failed to get his theory of states' authority over Indians accepted by Presidents Monroe and Adams. When he became President, Jackson maintained this position in spite of Constitutional treaty rights of the federal government. When this position was successfully challenged before the Supreme Court, Jackson simply refused to carry out the decision of the Court; in effect he "vetoed" the Court's decision. Following this, a series of state laws were passed which practically destroyed all Indian rights. Jackson ordered the Indians to move and provided federal funds to help transport them across the Mississippi. At one point, private contracts were given to buy them food and pay the costs of their removal, an arrangement which was obviously open to many varieties of corruption. Because of administration, it was impossible for Indians to protect even the rights which were given them under state laws. The result of this combination of circumstances was to make available most of the land in the South and Northwest to white settlers.

In domestic affairs, Jackson demonstrated Presidential authority by threatening the use of military force against South Carolina, which had moved to nullify an act of Congress by vetoing the Congressional act extending the charter of the Second Bank of the U.S., by challenging Congressional authority over the Secretary of the Treasury, and by using his appointing power to provide patronage to his supporters.

President Polk used his Presidential powers as commander-in-chief to encourage General Santa Ana's rebellion against the Mexican government through authorization of financial loans. Polk hoped that Santa Ana, having refitted his army, would negotiate transfer of land to the U.S. in payment. However, Mexican national pride made this impossible, and the Mexican War resulted. The United States victory in this war led to the annexation of the California Territory. In negotiations with Great Britain over the Oregon Territories, President Polk was subject to heavy pressure from the public, as well as the Congress, which demanded that he declare war in an attempt to gain the whole Territory. Polk was skilled enough, however, to get his treaty approved in spite of the fact that the area which he secured for the United States was much more limited than the "hawks" desired. Domestically, Polk succeeded in establishing the Treasury as the center of national monetary policy while the Congress was still trying to establish a new Bank. He also helped pass a tariff bill which was generally accepted. (Jackson had had a great battle with South Carolina over such a tariff.)

As we look for evidence of Presidential leadership in the years following Polk's Presidency, it is hard to find. Congress dominated this period of phenomenal growth. Accompanying the expanding boundaries and population of the United States were the extension of the railroads into the West and South, the industrial growth of the North and the burgeoning cotton plantation system of the South. Slavery was the major issue over which the union was divided; it was an economic as well as a social and moral issue.

In the issue of the expansion of slavery into new territories, the Compromise of 1850 was one Congressional attempt to solve the problem. The earlier Missouri Compromise of 1817 had admitted Missouri as a slave state and prohibited slavery in the rest of the Louisiana Purchase territory. The new proposal admitted California as a free state and specified that when the two territories of New Mexico and Arizona were ready to be admitted as states, there would be no restrictions placed upon them as to the existence of slavery. Congress also abolished the slave trade in the District of Columbia and plassed a drastic fugitive slave law. In 1854, these issues were re-opened in the proposals of the Kansas-Nebraska Act which gave each of these territories the right to decide whether slavery would be permitted. The complexity of the issue can be noted when it is realized that the principal proponent of the measure, Senator Stephen A. Douglas, was anxious to get the government of these territories settled to promote a railroad scheme in which he was interested. Southern senators attempted to block him, since they hoped that the extension of the railroad system would follow a southern route. In the "compromise," "squatter sovereignty" for new territories was traded for the railroad development on the northern route. The struggle over the Kansas-Nebraska Act was an important example of the way in which slavery affected Presidential politics by dividing Democrats as well as Republicans. Buchanan, the last of the northern Democrats, had refused to face the issues, but when the seceding South moved on Ft. Sumter, events moved the country to civil war.

LINCOLN AND JOHNSON

Abraham Lincoln and Andrew Johnson are of unusual importance in the development of the office of the President. In the continuing struggle between Congress and the President, Lincoln was successful and Johnson was a tragic failure. The issues around which their tenures of office centered were the place of blacks in American society, the extent of Presidential (vs. Congressional or judicial) power, and the relative strength of the states vs. the federal government.

Civil War in the United States was a struggle between two conflicting cultures. The culture of the North was one of the expanding ownership by whites into the newly opened territories and the growth of an industrial and commercial society in the East. In both instances, the free white workmen were ambitious and striving to build their own position in an expanding society. By contrast, the Southern society was dominated by a stagnant plantation economy with black slave labor. A substratum of "poor whites," little better off economically than the slaves, provided an additional characteristic of the Southern society. In the years before the Civil War, the expansion into new lands had, many times, forced a confrontation with the question: should the new lands be slave or free? This was not just a question of whether slavery was to be legal; there was an underlying fear on the part of whites that black slave labor would hold down the value of white free labor. The North feared the influx of free black labor as much as slave labor. This fear was compounded by the social segregation which separated whites and blacks, preventing either group from understanding the other. One needs only to read the political speeches of the North at the time to appreciate how little understanding there was of blacks as people rather than as slaves who were of a lower human order. Was it possible for two vastly different cultures represented by North and South to continue to live together as part of the same nation? This had been possible, but only by accepting the institution of slavery in the South and keeping blacks out of the North.

Lincoln and Johnson had to find their places as Presidents within these conflicting social realms. Lincoln's position on the issue of slavery was well-known. He had said that the nation could not last half-slave and half-free, but he had also said that he was prepared to compromise on this issue if the Union could be preserved. Johnson's, too, was well-known. He had been a Democrat and a Unionist and, during the war, a vigorous military governor of Tennessee; but these attitudes had to change as the war went on.

Lincoln came into office knowing that the Confederacy had already been formed, the representatives of the Southern states had withdrawn from Congress and Ft. Sumter had already been attacked. Congress was not in session and Lincoln's first moves could have been challenged for going beyond his powers: he issued a call for volunteers and he authorized the expenditure of funds for supplies, both without prior Congressional approval. As time went on, Lincoln continued to assume and successfully use more powers. He blocked the attempts in Congress to appoint generals and control the conduct of the war, he declared a blockade against Southern ports and he declared martial law. Furthermore, he refused to recognize the issuance of a writ of *habeas corpus* when issued by the Chief Justice of the Supreme Court.

The most important of Lincoln's actions under his powers as commander-in-chief, was his issuance of the Emancipation Proclamation. This action was important not only in freeing slaves but also in changing attitudes in Europe where the debate on recognition of the Confederacy was going on. Throughout the long, bitter, bloody struggle over slavery, Lincoln succeeded in holding his public support by toughness, combined with skill, humility, and a sense of compassion.

Andrew Johnson's Presidency is tragic from many points of view. He was a Democratic Unionist in a border state when to be so required loyalty and courage. After the war, this sense of unity required that the Southern states be promptly readmitted to national government and that their powers be restored. However, he was opposed by an overwhelmingly powerful Congress which regarded itself as victor over traitors. Johnson's sense of the Constitutional powers of the President were directly in conflict with those of the Congress, and his attempts to secure Supreme Court rulings on the locus of powers failed when the Court refused to accept jurisdiction.

Johnson's weakness as President stemmed from the fact that he had been chosen as Vice-President, not as President. He had been part of the Lincoln-Johnson ticket and represented a point of view which was essential to Lincoln's objectives in seeking re-election. Johnson was part of the Republican Party's strategy for building a broader base, since Lincoln had been elected originally by only a minority of voters.

When Johnson became President after Lincoln's assassination, his attempts to use the powers of his office were overruled at every step. Southern congressmen, chosen according to the steps originally proposed by Lincoln under his wartime authority, were not admitted by Congress, which is the judge of its own membership. When Congress passed laws continuing the Freedman's Bureau, which had been established under military rule to provide assistance for the freed slaves, Johnson vetoed them. He also vetoed laws providing for the establishment of full political rights for negroes. Both of these were promptly passed over the veto. When the election for new Congressional members was under way in 1867, Johnson tried to use his influence to secure a more compatible Congress. The new Congress, however, was equally determined to continue Reconstruction in the South. The President handled the division of the South into military districts in a way which made the military governors feel that they need not be responsible to him. Stanton, Johnson's Secretary of War, although a minority of one in the cabinet, refused to carry out his instructions. Furthermore, Congress passed the Tenure of Office Act which limited the President's authority to dismiss without Senatorial consent officials who had been nominated by the President and approved by Congress. In addition, Congress specifically prohibited the President from using his power as commander-in-chief to control the military governors in the South. Finally, the conflicts between Johnson and Congress led to impeachment proceedings in the House. However, the impeachment failed by one vote of the two-thirds required to convict in the Senate.

The contrast of the Presidencies of Lincoln and Johnson could hardly be sharper. Under Lincoln it was obvious that the President was able to carry out actions which were Constitutionally questionable. Lincoln followed a principle established by Jefferson and Jackson, a principle which Jefferson, at the time of the Louisiana Purchase, had called the law "of necessity of self-preservation, of saving the country when in danger." Under Johnson, the President was prevented from exercising even those powers which were specifically given him by the Constitution. The Supreme Court's refusal to assume jurisdiction in the most flagrant cases made the issue clearly one of political power.

As the country entered the era of Reconstruction, following the war, the dominant issue was that of state versus federal power. Congress was determined that the states return to the Union under terms decided in

Washington. The Thirteenth, Fourteenth, and Fifteenth Amendments were passed, not only to prohibit slavery, but also to establish this authority beyond question. While the Constitutional basis for federal supremacy was established, it was to pass into disuse in segregation cases and was not to be revived until almost a century later. The dominance of the Congress over the President, established during Johnson's term of office, was to continue when Grant became President.

GRANT TO MCKINLEY

During the period from Grant to McKinley, America experienced an unparalleled period of expansion and growth. The westward push of the railroads opened the Great Plains to development, and agriculture and industry flourished. As the economy grew, the potential for advancement attracted immigrants who, in turn, provided the work force for further growth.

The availability of economic opportunities produced the Age of the Robber Barons. The political movements (growing out of agriculture and labor) which might have pushed for reforms, were never strong enough to overcome the growth of corporate power. Congress was friendly to big business and the Supreme Court rendered judgments which established a legal framework for corporate expansion and development. The roles which Congress and the Courts assumed left the President, except as a dispenser of patronage, in a place of secondary importance.

In spite of the pervasive belief that freedom for private business and limited governmental control were the ways in which the country should develop, the growth of the country demanded the growth of government. The distribution of land and other resources, the need for new roads, the growth of the communications network—particularly the postal service—and the need for expanded public services in the cities, all required the expansion of government.

From the time of President Jackson, government jobs had been regarded as one of the foundations of political parties. Under the Constitution, the President was authorized to make appointments with the advice and consent of the Senate. In practice, Presidential struggles over patronage were time consuming and prevented attention to more important issues. Consequently, the Presidents sought new ways to select government employees.

There were numerous steps along the road to the Civil Service Commission which finally came into existence in 1883. Prior to this there had been small appropriations for examinations for a few selected civil service employees, and after Congress discontinued these appropriations some departments gave their own examinations. The final step which led to the Civil Service Commission was taken only after the nation was shocked by President Garfield's assassination by a demented job seeker.

When Grant became President, the Congress controlled him as much as it had controlled President Johnson. Grant made a few feeble efforts to assert himself and then surrendered completely; he had been a great general but was a most naïve President. Congress' control of appointees had been further strengthened by the Tenure of Office Act. Johnson had unsuccessfully attempted to veto this Act and Grant was tied hand and foot by it, as was every succeeding President, until it was abolished during Cleveland's Presidency in 1887.

The election of Grant's successor, Rutherford B. Hayes had been made possible by a "deal" in which some Republican officials in Florida and Louisiana had tampered with the vote count, in return for patronage. In an attempt to prevent Southern Democrats from taking strong actions based upon their knowledge of this situation, he agreed to terminate military rule in their states and to make adequate patronage available to their constituencies. After settling these scores, Hayes reversed course and fought to regain control over his appointments.

Hayes was succeeded by James A. Garfield whose Presidency was very prematurely ended by his assassination. When Vice-President Chester A. Arthur succeeded Garfield, he surprised a great many people by his insistence upon maintaining the dignity of the office. Although he had been part of the Customs House machine in New York City, he demonstrated a high degree of independence in making appointments, and it was during his administration that the Civil Service Commission was established.

Although President Cleveland was a Democrat, as opposed to the succession of Republicans who had preceded him, it is notable that there was little fundamental change in Presidential policies under his administration. He continued to push for civil service reform, and, having had little national political experience, he sought out qualified people for all significant appointments. He vetoed many bills which would have distributed unearned favors. It must be remembered that, even though merit had become an important element in federal appointments, there were still thousands of jobs at the President's disposal.

In the realm of substantive policy, during the period from Grant to McKinley, the President and the other branches of government all agreed that the encouragement of corporate power was the principal means for bringing economic development to the country. In the monetary field, there was consistent Presidential support for the gold standard. The agrarians and others who were sensitive to the downward pressure of gold on price levels tried to introduce an inflationary force into the monetary system by requiring the introduction of free silver into the system; but their attempts had only limited success over Presidential opposition.

In the field of foreign affairs, it was clear that Presidential power was limited. Grant was successful in negotiating the settlement of claims against the British for capture of merchant vessels by Southern ships built in British shipyards, and Cleveland was successful in securing the arbitration of the Venezuela dispute with Great Britain. However, when Grant attempted to secure Senatorial approval for annexation of Santa Domingo, his efforts failed.

During President William McKinley's term, the issue of Congressional as against Presidential power hardly arose. McKinley had had long experience in, and knowledge of, the Congress, and the Congress and the President saw eye to eye on most issues. On one major issue, however, there was a difference of judgment. President McKinley opposed the United States becoming involved in the revolution taking place in Cuba. Congress saw it otherwise and prominent newspapers helped to create a ground swell of public opinion for war with Spain. McKinley finally succumbed to Congressional and public pressure and the Spanish-American War was the result. Thus, the United States became an imperial power, a posture which was further established by annexation of Hawaii and the Phillipines and by participation in an international expedition to Peking at the time of the Boxer uprising against foreigners.

When McKinley was assassinated, Vice-President Theodore Roosevelt succeeded him. The imperialistic policies begun under McKinley were to be reinforced by Roosevelt who had planned for the Spanish-American War and had also participated in the Cuban invasion with his Rough Riders.

THEODORE ROOSEVELT TO HOOVER

The era between the two Roosevelts produced two strong Presidents—Theodore Roosevelt and Woodrow Wilson—and four weak Presidents—Taft (who followed Roosevelt), Harding (who followed Wilson), Coolidge and Hoover.

Theodore Roosevelt's efforts to establish the United States as an imperialistic world power must be seen as part of a larger trend of the times. European governments were trying to expand their imperial power to match that of Great Britain and even Great Britain was moving to expand its empire still further. France and Italy were expanding into Africa; King William II of Prussia had become Kaiser of Germany and was determined to demonstrate that Germany too was an imperial power. The mutual admiration which Roosevelt and the Kaiser had for each other was well-known; both believed in the show, as well as the substance, of power. Roosevelt ordered the American fleet on a world-wide tour to exhibit this country's power even though at the time no funds had been authorized to finance this display. After Roosevelt took this action, Congress appropriated funds to bring the fleet home.

Roosevelt took many vigorous actions in foreign affairs. In one instance he forced Santa Domingo to pay the interest on its debts by occupying the customs house and taking charge of Dominican funds. He covered his action with an executive agreement which the Senate at first challenged as in violation of his powers, but later approved. In another situation he successfully challenged Germany's threat to occupy the Venezuelan customs house to force interest payments due to European bond holders. Roosevelt's initiation of the arbitration proceedings for settlement of the Russo-Japanese War was acknowledged by his being awarded the Nobel prize, but the action which gave him greatest personal pride was the building of the Panama Canal. Both Nicaragua and Columbia were anxious to have a canal and there had been support in Congress for the canal for a long time before Roosevelt became President. When Roosevelt felt that negotiations were being "held up" by Columbia, he encouraged and supported the independence of Panama from Columbia and then secured the treaty which permitted the canal to be built.

All of this vigorous action was matched in the domestic field. While Roosevelt was not convinced of the evil of "bigness" he was determined to enforce the anti-trust laws. He won the famous Northern Securities anti-trust case which involved a consolidation of Union Pacific and Northern Pacific railroad interests. This case was successfully followed by prosecutions which resulted in dissolution of the Standard Oil Trust and the Tobacco Trust. Roosevelt soon learned, however, that these cases did not have the desired results. It was easier to spot monopoly than to create competition.

Roosevelt was prepared to take equally vigorous steps in dealing with a long drawn-out coal strike in eastern Pennyslvania in the spring of 1902. He first attempted to mediate but found management completely unwilling to face the union. After long and complicated political discussions with the state authorities, he threatened to seize the mines and operate them as a receiver unless there was a settlement; the strike was settled.

Having served most of McKinley's term, as well as his own, Roosevelt refused to run for a third term and instead was able to secure the nomination of one of his most trusted associates, William Howard Taft. After his election it became evident that Taft's own philosophy of the Presidency went along with the standard idea that the office of the President was one of administering the laws and following the policies laid down by the Congress. Roosevelt, whose joy had been in using the office as an opportunity to lead, was so saddened by Taft's performance that he decided to run again. When he was rejected by the Republican Convention, he left the party and helped establish the Progressive Party. The result was a split in the electorate and Woodrow Wilson's election as President.

While Wilson's style was very different than that of Roosevelt, both men shared the belief that the President should provide strong leadership for the country. Wilson believed that "leadership" meant understanding where the great mass of people wanted to go, and being at the head of that procession. He had pursued studies of history and government in depth and he had become a great believer in the British system of parliamentary government. As President, he saw himself as a Prime Minister who must work with the legislature. He believed that the separation of powers is, in itself, insufficient to provide an operating system of government. Wilson demonstrated, as only a few Presidents have, that he could work with Congress, particularly with a Congress of his own party. He revived the process of going in person to the Capitol, he used the party caucus and he dealt directly with party leaders. Wilson used patronage when it

was necessary to persuade and he demonstrated that he could be a "political" manager of great skill. If his academic background had provided him with insufficient "practical" experience, his service as President of Princeton University and his Governorship of New Jersey had given him adequate experience in academic and state politics.

Wilson's political skills enabled him to secure passage of a bill lowering the tariff, anti-trust laws (the Clayton and Federal Trade Commission Acts), and the Federal Reserve Act. Corporation growth, concentration of economic power, and monopoly controlled prices continued in spite of anti-trust legislation and attempts to introduce a greater degree of competition. The Federal Reserve Act was an attempt, by Wilson and Congress, to answer the great demand for monetary reform. They hoped that it would provide greater flexibility in the monetary system and would guarantee more integrity in the operation of the banks.

Although Wilson had been re-elected on a slogan of "he kept us out of war," a long series of struggles with the British and the Germans over the rights of ships of neutral powers were never solved and eventually drew the United States into World War I. At first, the United States saw its role in the war as an "arsenal for democracy." There was a rapid awarding of contracts which led to some notorious scandals such as the unfulfilled promise of the motor industry to produce aircraft engines. The Congress, as it had during previous periods, began to talk of a Congressional committee to run the war. Wilson made a counterproposal, to which the Congress finally agreed, giving the President powers to reorganize the government to promote the efficient conduct of the war. He also established a Selective Service System, successfully overcoming strong opposition which preferred a volunteer system.

President Wilson made a very important and unique contribution to the way in which Americans viewed the war. Before America's entry into the war, the war had been seen solely as a European struggle for power. When Wilson proclaimed that this was a war "to make the world safe for democracy," he provided an idealistic framework for this country's military and material involvement in the war. In his famous Fourteen Points speech, Wilson called for justice for small nations, self-determination for enslaved peoples and arbitration before war. These goals were embraced by Americans of many persuasions and they became one of the most powerful instruments for destroying morale in Germany and Japan. The Fourteen Points speech derived particular strength from the integrity of its author; it was an extremely persuasive state document. While it played an important role in the recognition of the independent eastern European nations after the war, there were other parts of the world in which it was not endorsed. Japan, for example, didn't accept it as applying to the Asian mainland and western European governments didn't read it as applying to their colonies.

Wilson's attempts to incorporate his ideals into the settlement which followed the war met with little success. When he realized that his efforts had been blocked by Lloyd George, Clemenceau and Orlando—the three leaders of the European allied nations—he retreated and tried, instead, to secure an agreement to establish the League of Nations as the framework within which further attempts could be made to secure his wartime objectives. However, he had gone to Paris to try to negotiate after the election of 1918 in which he had lost his majorities

in both houses of Congress, and he found himself caught in a parliamentary web of his own creation. Under a parliamentary system he would have had to resign when his party lost an election. Instead, he abandoned his earlier convictions that the President must work with Congress and when Congress refused to accept his agreement for a League of Nations made while in Europe, he started an appeal to the people, convinced that he could rally their support. In the middle of this effort, however, he suffered a physical collapse and was never to regain the capacity to continue his term in office with any degree of competence. During the final years of his Presidency the people were deprived of any real leadership from the White House or Congress.

The three Presidents who followed Wilson reflected a different sense of the functions of the Presidency. Harding, whose rallying cry was "back to normalcy," was followed by Coolidge and then Hoover, neither of whom showed strong leadership. The Presidency was seen as an office to carry out policies decided upon by Congress, a concept of government that requires that the Presidents make strong administrative appointments. President Harding did not choose the best men to serve him. His friends betrayed him, the full extent of their venality becoming known only after his death. Harding's lax attitude towards his responsibilities was also clear in his handling of foreign affairs. The Senate Committee on Foreign Relations had to practically force him to call the Washington Naval Conference, the one significant foreign relations event of his Presidency.

During Harding's term, freedom of enterprise had made no distinction between legal and illegal enterprise, and the early years of the Presidency of his successor, Calvin Coolidge, were notable for the prosecution of corruption between businessmen and high government officials. Coolidge was convinced that the less the President did, the better off the country would be, and that the government should minimize its control of economic activity by maintaining the status quo in regards to existing governmental controls.

President Herbert Hoover continued the relaxed attitude of his two predecessors. In one sense this attitude was appropriate. The economy was booming and, while there were areas of poverty, the potential for improving the lives of all citizens seemed available. Since World War I, the international interdependence of the economy had been becoming more and more apparent. Hoover had wide international experience. As Secretary of Commerce for Coolidge, he had built one of the ablest federal bureaus, the Bureau of Foreign and Domestic Commerce. He had also been an engineer in China and Australia and had served as a relief administrator in Europe following World War I. All of this experience, it seems, might have made him highly sensitive to clouds on the international horizon. However, he, like other world leaders of the time, failed to anticipate the true significance of economic interdependency.

The collapse of the stock market in 1929 was followed by the prolonged depression which seemed to call for governmental actions. European nations regarded the international phenomenon as something to be dealt with by nationalist measures. First Italy's Fascism and then Germany's National Socialism were the popular solutions. In the United States, however, Hoover remained convinced that natural forces would revive the economy and took little action. He felt that relief functions were the responsibility of the states. During the Presidential election, Hoover ran on a conservative plat-

form, convinced that recovery was imminent, while Franklin D. Roosevelt believed that strong domestic actions were essential; neither was sensitive to the international facets of the problem. In the four month interim between Roosevelt's election and his assuming office, he was unwilling to work with Hoover in developing recovery programs, even though the depression continued to worsen. The decline of the Presidency, however, was to end dramatically with Roosevelt's administration.

F. D. ROOSEVELT TO FORD

With hindsight it is easy to see that Roosevelt's reorganization of the office of the President marks a major change in the Presidency. Roosevelt and Truman were to set the pattern for their successors. During Eisenhower's Presidency, the leadership seemed to shift to Congress, but Kennedy, Johnson, Nixon and Ford accepted the pattern of Presidential leadership. Each has had his successes and failures, but all, except Nixon, have shown the respect which is demanded of the office.

The highly organized office which Roosevelt and Truman left to their successors was not neatly planned; it grew out of the demands of new programs which had previously been assumed to be the responsibility of the states or of private business. The times had demanded emergency relief, public works, agricultural relief, rural electrification, industrial subsidy, trade union and consumer organization, housing and monetary reform, and reform of the security markets. Although these programs had to be carried out by new agencies, both Roosevelt and Truman believed that the President should supervise them. Although they recognized the roles of the Congress and the Supreme Court, they believed that the President also must accept responsibility for solving the country's problems.

When Roosevelt found that his cabinet was not a satisfactory body for handling new activities, he asked a group of administrative specialists to help him. Their most important recommendation, the establishment of the Executive Office of the President, was accepted by the Congress. The Executive Office of the President was separated from the President's personal office, the White House. Up to this time the Presidents had been severely limited in the number of assistants they had; now a small group of assistants became formalized. Substance was added by the transfer of the Budget Bureau (now the Office of Management and Budget) to the Executive Office. Today, the Office of Management and Budget is one of the most important of the President's working tools.

With the advent of World War II, Roosevelt expanded his staff with a special Military Aide and with other assistants to help him administer the multitude of wartime agencies authorized under the War Powers Acts. Following the war, under the Truman administration, Congress strengthened the Executive Office of the President still further by approving proposals for two major additions: the National Security Council and the Council of Economic Advisors. The National Security Council was composed of the President, the Secretary of State, the Secretary of Defense (Army, Navy and Air Force) and the Central Intelligence Agency, which was created to bring order into reports from the numerous intelligence agencies. The Council of Economic Advisors was created to help the President make recommendations to Congress regarding ways to maintain high level employment. Another major additon to the Executive Office, President Nixon's Domestic Council, was established to give the same attention to domestic affairs as that given to foreign affairs by the National Security Council. President Kennedy added the National Aeronautics and Space Council, and President Johnson added the Office of Economic Opportunity.

Roosevelt's administration can be roughly divided into two periods. Prior to the war Roosevelt had given little attention to foreign affairs. He had instituted a Good Neighbor Policy vis a vis Latin America, a reciprocal international trade policy, and he had recognized the USSR. After these major acts, he turned his attention inward. During this period, Roosevelt's concerns were with emergency relief and recovery, and with long term programs which established Social Security, monetary and banking regulations, housing finance programs, welfare legislation and the definition of trade union rights. The second period of Roosevelt's administration was dominated by World War II, during which the federal government assumed control of practically every phase of economic life in order to maximize the military power of the country. Before and during World War II, the Department of State played a relatively minor role, while most of the significant decisions were made in the office of the President. After the war, the world looked to the United States for assistance and leadership and much of this demand was focused upon the President.

The demands of the Cold War, which followed World War II, continued to focus responsibility on the President. However, President Truman no longer had the tremendous Congressional support that had existed during World War II. The collapse of China under Chiang Kai-shek's leadership to the People's Republic had polarized relations inside the United Nations and attitudes within the United States and, during the Cold War, the Presidency was often under attack by Congress for not making the Cold War more vigorous. (This was true not only under President Truman, but also under President Eisenhower.) While some of this was in the nature of partisan politics, the bitterness extended to accusing the President of traitorous conduct. The power of the Presidency was never more clearly demonstrated than when President Truman responded to his struggles with General MacArthur by dismissing him, in spite of the fact that MacArthur had much support from Congress.

The Presidency was strengthened still further by Truman's careful and skillful handling of his Congressional relations in the establishment of the Marshall Plan. This plan, to assist reconstruction in western Europe, involved huge appropriations over a long period of time and, without Congressional support, it would have been impossible to achieve. Senator Vandenburg, a Republican, joined Truman and helped him to get the necessary votes from Congress. In return, Vandenburg insisted that an independent agency which was, in effect, a second State Department, be instituted to administer the Marshall Plan. While administrative duplication complicated the President's problems, the acceptance of the plan was a major victory for the President.

The Cold War was made more difficult by the introduction of a new factor, the atomic bomb. The bomb had been developed in great secrecy during World War II and its use, against Japan, demonstrated its ghastly possibilities. President Truman's attempt to find a method of bringing nuclear power under international control was unsuccessful. His proposal for a United Nations Atomic Energy Commission was not adopted. The USSR insisted upon maintaining its own program of nuclear development and long drawn-out negotiations over the intervening years have not yet produced a satisfactory solution to this problem.

Following the war, the international relief and development programs undertaken on Presidential initiative became involved in the Cold War. On the military side, the alliance of European nations in N.A.T.O., the Korean War. President Eisenhower's "open skies" proposal, the continuing recognition of a Chinese government on the island of Taiwan as the government of "China," and the involvement from Truman to Nixon in the Vietnam War, all testified to the growing power of the Presidents. Truman's use of his power to recognize Israel also emphasized Presidential power. More recently, Nixon's reversal of long standing policy in the Far East by his recognition of the People's Republic of China in the United Nations, and his development of a policy of detente in relation to the Soviet Union, have shown what Presidents can do with their powers in foreign policy.

Where the actions just cited are examples of the power which Presidents can use in foreign affairs, it must also be noted that some actions have had the opposite effect. The failure of Truman and his successors to negotiate an international agreement for control of atomic energy has emphasized the limits of Presidential power. The effect of Eisenhower and Kennedy's badly conceived and administered Bay of Pigs venture was only partially offset by the success in preventing the placements of nuclear weapons in Cuba. The continued failure of many Presidents in the Vietnam War reflected badly on the Presidency as well as on the nation. It should be noted that the Congress reacted to national opinion concerning Vietnam more quickly than the Presidents.

In domestic affairs as well as foreign, Roosevelt and Truman were sensitive to the direction in which the country wished to go. Roosevelt accepted the goal of "full employment," but achieved it only during World War II, although it was not one of the objectives of the war. In spite of the fact that Truman was confronted with the problems of an over-employed economy, neither he nor Congress had difficulty in accepting the Full Employment Act of 1946, an act which placed the goal of "full employment" in the lap of the President. The President and Congress are still trying to achieve this goal and even the lack of success of the past few years has not redounded to the discredit of the Presidency. The American public has exhibited a remarkable understanding of the difficulties inherent in this attempt.

In the climate of post World War II, continuing racial discrimination created demands for change. President Truman took one major step by executive action to desegregate both the civil service and the military service. Successive Presidents have continued to actively support the Supreme Court's leadership in this field. President Eisenhower, however, intervened powerfully in the Little Rock school desegregation case, and even opponents of such action have agreed that the Presidency has been strengthened when Presidents have insisted that the status of racial minorities must be equal to that of the white majority.

Presidential support of an expanding Tennessee Valley Authority and other rural electrification and multipurpose water projects, as well as the post-war federal interstate road program and conservation activities has also strenthened the Presidency. In spite of these federal programs, the area of public works still retains an element of "pork barrelling."

The agricultural programs initiated by President Roosevelt have been almost universally championed by succeeding Presidents. When there has been hesitation by a President, the Congress has usually insisted on the continuation of federally subsidized agriculture.

Most of the forward steps in public welfare have redounded to the credit of the Presidency; they have been initiated and continuously supported by the Presidents and have been given momentum in the Congress. Among these, social security, unemployment insurance and public assistance have expanded steadily. Medical insurance for the aged and the poor were pushed through the Congress by Presidents Kennedy and Johnson and President Nixon expanded the experimental food stamp program to a national program costing billions. Nixon also transferred some responsibility for categorical relief to the states but his attempt to institute a guaranteed minimum income was blocked in a Senate committee.

The Presidency has increasingly been seen as a source of leadership for national programs, but this movement has not been all steadily forward. In the early days of the New Deal Roosevelt had received support from the Congress, but the Supreme Court interposed strong inhibitions upon him and only after the bitter "court packing" struggle did the Court change its judgment as to what was Constitutional. In the later New Deal days, the Congress, too, set up many obstacles and the President had to employ various strategies to secure the legislation that he believed the country wanted. President Truman's leadership was exerted continuously, but was often rejected by Congress. In addition, he was rebuffed by the Supreme Court when he seized some steel mills which were on strike, an action which he regarded as within his "war powers" incident to the Korean War. The Supreme Court under Chief Justice Warren's guidance also overshadowed the Presidency in a long series of decisions which sought to rectify the Presidents' failure to carry out laws which had been on the books since the passage of Constitutional amendments and statutes following the Civil War. President Nixon also was challenged by the Congress and the Supreme Court in his decisions regarding two appointments to the Supreme Court. His choices reflected poor staff work on extremely important decisions and Congress rejected them as being cavalier. Nixon's later appointments indicated greater sensitivity to Congress and to the Court's future membership.

The most fundamental challenge in modern times to the Presidency has already been referred to in reviewing the President's action in committing material in Vietnam. Whatever the Constitutionality of the President's position in foreign affairs, this authority cannot be sustained without the support of the public. Both Presidents Johnson and Nixon had tried to build public support but results in Vietnam were so bad that they both lost support they had originally had. Congress was sensitive to this loss of support before the Presidents themselves. The long delay in negotiations, started by President Johnson and carried out by President Nixon, came to reflect unfavorably on the Presidency itself. In the case of Nixon, the public bitterness became so great that he tended to withdraw almost completely from the public. When illegalities in the financing of Nixon's reelection campaign and the subsequent cover-up attempts became known, they were seen as attempts to expand the powers of the President beyond Constitutional limits, and he was forced to resign. Both Congress and the Supreme Court, reflecting public outrage, destroyed what Nixon called his "political support."

President Ford came into office with a major assignment: to re-establish the integrity of the Presidency and the credibility of the United States. Ford's pardon of Nixon's possible crimes removed these actions from public controversy and his restaffing of the White House (retaining only those high officials concerning whom there was no controversy), enabled the government to move forward. The ultimate success of the new President has yet to be established.

In the history of America, each of the three parts of the federal government has claimed that it had Constitutional powers over the other two. The Court has asserted its right to overrule both the President and the Congress. The Congress has said that it has the right to "legislate" and to overturn decisions of the Court. The President has made his claim that, when faced with emergencies, he has powers which supersede those of either the Court or the Congress. The problem of distinguishing between legislative, administrative and judicial definitions of national interest is insoluble in the abstract. From time to time in the two hundred years of this country's Constitutional existence each has been successful in having its view of the "will of the people" supported by the other branches of government. We are living in a period when the necessity for quality in all three branches was never more apparrent.

Cartoons

Artist Unknown. "The Times, a Political Portrait". (1797). Engraving. 12¼ × 17¾". Collection The New-York Historical Society, New York, New York.

*

No copy remains of "The Entry," the only cartoon of George Washington known to have appeared during his first term as President. Published in April 1789, at the time of his first inauguration, it pictured Washington riding into the nation's capital, New York, on an ass. It was, of course, obviously uncomplimentary to the famous American who had so often been idealized in a classic equestrian pose atop his white steed.

This Federalist cartoon, "The Times, a Political Portrait," shows Washington in a much more sympathetic light. Atop a chariot drawn by two horses, flanked on each side by the volunteers recruited during the Whiskey Rebellion, Washington is triumphantly defending justice (note the caption) against French Republican "cannibals" and French Revolutionary sympathizers. While Thomas Jefferson attempts to "stop the wheels of government," Benjamin Franklin Bache, editor of the Republican newspaper *Aurora* and grandson of the Philadelphia patroit, is trampled by the soldiers while a dog lifts a leg on his paper. In the left background, the Federalist eagle strikes the approaching cannibals, aiding Washington in halting the spread of Robespierre's terror.

When he assumed the Presidency, Washington had several major tasks ahead of him. One of these tasks was the necessity, as Washington saw it, of making clear the President's complete assumption of responsibility for foreign affairs. When France declared war on England in 1793, Washington demonstrated his special responsibilities as President by issuing a neutrality proclamation. This was a difficult stand, not only because there was an old treaty of alliance with France dating from the American Revolution, but because the Congress—convinced that the President had usurped its powers—violently protested. In spite of the protests Washington stood firm.   G.B.

Triumph Government: perish all its enemies._

Traitors, be warned: justice though slow, is sure.

Artist Unknown. "The Providential Detection". (c. 1797). Line engraving. 16¼ × 14". Collection The Library Company of Philadelphia.

*

In the cartoon, Thomas Jefferson kneels before the altar of Gallic despotism and kindles a sacrificial fire with the works of such controversial European minds as William Godwin, Jean Rousseau, and Claude Helvetius. He is stopped short from burning the Constitution by the American eagle, stalwart defender of the federal republic. Startled by the attack, Jefferson drops his scandalous letter to Philip Mazzei, in which he accused the Federalists of being "Samsons in the field and Solomons in the Council...who have had their heads shorn by the harlot of England."

This cartoon was originally dated 1800 by Murrell, Nevins and Weitenkampf. In a more recent study, however, Gordon N. Marshall of the Library Company of Philadelphia claims that the issues depicted were of greater significance during the election of 1796, in which Jefferson was defeated by Adams. If Marshall is correct, "The Providential Detection" can be seen as a "celebration" of Adams' election and the rescue of America from internal disorder. It expresses the Federalist belief that if Jefferson became President, his radical thinking would endanger the Constitution.

It is interesting to note that Jefferson feared the Federalist philosophy just as much as they feared his. Jefferson believed that the Federalist Presidents, Washington and Adams, had assumed too much control— control which rightfully belonged to Congress. This was ironic, for when Jefferson became President, his subtle control over Congress re-emphasized the powers of that office.   G.B.

THE PROVIDENTIAL DETECTION

Artist Unknown. "Mad Tom in a Rage".
(1801?). Etching and ink on blue paper.
2$\frac{1}{16}$ × 7". Collection Houghton Library,
Harvard University, Cambridge, Mass.

*

In this broadsheet cartoon engraved c. 1801,
an unknown artist depicts a devil with highly individualized features aiding a man
named Tom in pulling down a column. The
letters "FEDL GOVRN," "G. WAS" and
"J. ADA" inscribed on the column clearly
indicate the Federalist party.

"Mad Tom in a Rage" seems to be an attack
on President Thomas Jefferson's association
with Thomas Paine. The President's friendship with Paine was not well received
among the Federalists, who considered the
revolutionary pamphleteer anarchistic. Yet
the cartoon is problematic in that it is not
certain which man—Jefferson or Paine—is
"Tom." Speculations have ranged in both
directions, yet the presence of the brandy
bottle, the manuscripts stuffed in Tom's
pocket, and the defined facial features suggest that Thomas Paine is the more likely
of the two. Paine was rumored to have had
a drinking problem and, unlike Jefferson,
his political writings were widely published
at the time. Tom's face also strongly resem-
bles the portrait of Thomas Paine by George
Romney. The devil may indeed represent
Jefferson, Tom's "Old Friend."   L.K.

MAD TOM IN A RAGE

Artist Unknown. "Look on this Picture,
and on This". 1807. Line engraving.
9$\frac{3}{16}$ × 12$\frac{1}{4}$". Collection The New-York
Historical Society, New York, New York.

*

"Look on this Picture, and on This" is
another attack on President Jefferson's character. Published as a separate broadsheet,
this highly sophisticated caricature com-
pares President Jefferson unfavorably with
the legendary Washington. By using tondo
portraits, animals which traditionally symbolize certain human characteristics, and
appropriate verses, this cartoonist cleverly
juxtaposes corresponding representations
of good and evil.

Above Washington a laurel-halo emits rays
of eternal light, while over Jefferson a can-
dle smolders. A majestic lion and an American eagle stand on either side of a pyramid of volumes entitled "Order," "Law,"
and "Religion." In contrast, under Jefferson
a sinister lizard and a coiled snake pose next
to volumes labeled "Sophisms," "Notes on
Virginia," "Tom Paine," "Condorcet," and
"Voltaire."

The artist, unfortunately unidentifiable,
exhibits excellent draftsmanship in the
unusually accurate likenesses of the two
men. His broadsheet stands out as a particularly biting comment on Thomas
Jefferson.   L.K.

LOOK ON THIS PICTURE, AND ON THIS

LOOK ON THIS PICTURE, AND ON THIS.

"Peter Pencil". "Intercourse or Impartial Dealings". 1809. Etching and stipple printed with sepia ink. 10⅜ × 12¾". Collection Houghton Library, Harvard University, Cambridge, Mass.

*

"Peter Pencil(l)". "Non Intercourse or Dignified Retirement". 1809. Etching and stipple printed with sepia ink. 10¼ × 12⅝". Collection Houghton Library, Harvard University, Cambridge, Mass.

*

Though America attempted to maintain a neutral stance in the European war between England and France, she was nonetheless affected by it. For neither France nor England wanted the other to carry on trade with the United States, and both countries plundered American ships. Hoping to avoid a war with the two nations, President Jefferson signed the Embargo Acts, prohibiting American trade with either France or England. But what was intended as a punishment to these two European nations proved to be a great economic hardship to the United States, and the Embargo was repealed. It was replaced by the Non-Intercourse Act, a somewhat milder version of the same thing.

This pair of extremely fine copperplate impressions by "Peter Pencil" protests President Jefferson's Non-Intercourse Act. In the first cartoon, the artist expresses the President's "dealings" with these countries by depicting England (represented by King George III) and France (shown as Napoleon) robbing Jefferson. As the cartoon suggests, Jefferson is "impartial" in his treatment of the two countries. Yet the second print strongly implies that Jefferson's "Non-Intercourse" policy was not a voluntary act on the part of America, but a submission to French demands. (Note that Jefferson, at Napoleon's direction, takes off his shirt of Irish linen.)

The exquisite draftsmanship, evident in the expertly drawn lines and diverse shading and texture, belong to a highly skilled artist. Obviously acquainted with other cartoonists' works, "Peter Pencil" easily identifies his characters. The enlarged Napoleonic headpiece was a common motif used by other American artists, and the depiction of King George distinctly recalls those of the English Thomas Gillray, probably the most prominent cartoonist of the period. Judging from the unusually fine quality and sophistication of this cartoon, and comparing it with others printed by Americans during this time, it is not unlikely that "Peter Pencil" may have been trained abroad. L.K.

INTERCOURSE OR IMPARTIAL DEALINGS / NON INTERCOURSE OR DIGNIFIED RETIREMENT

INTERCOURSE or Impartial Dealings

NON INTERCOURSE or Dignified Retirement

Artist Unknown. "An Old Philosopher Teaching his Mad Son Economical Projects". (1809). Etching. 12⅞ × 17". Collection Free Library of Philadelphia.

*

This cartoon probably appeared in 1809, toward the end of Jefferson's Presidency. The advanced draftsmanship, conscious coloration, and style of the artist, suggest his English training and exposure to the works of eighteenth-century caricaturist, James Gillray.

Uniquely composed, this cartoon presents the story of the Embargo Bill, beginning in the lower left with the Chesapeake-Leopard incident of 1807. Here a British naval vessel, the Leopard, is seen attacking an American frigate, the Chesapeake. The third ship in the frame is cannonading the various acts of commercial warfare which America waged against England.

New England merchants saw the embargo legislation as a collusion with Emperor Napoleon. The large drawing captures the President and his accomplice, James Madison, hauling a ship into dock at the command of Bonaparte. Revealing his political motivations, Madison comments, "France wants an Embargo & must have it! Up with these Ships into the dry dock to preserve our resources. God send the Emperor may make me a President!"

Behind the scene a dissatisfied Congress debates the future of the Embargo. One dissident claims, "Everything is carefully concealed from us... My life upon it the hand of Napoleon is in this Embargo bill."

In the lower right cartoon an unrecognizable figure dangling before John Bull and Bonaparte appears to represent America's position during the embargo years.   G.B.

An Old Philosopher Teaching His Mad Son Economical Projects

Alexander Anderson. "To the Grave Go Sham Protectors of 'Free Trade and Sailors' Rights'—and All the People Say Amen!" (1814). Wood engraving. 7½ × 4¾". Collection Prints Division, The New York Public Library: Astor, Lenox and Tilden Foundations.

*

"Down to the grave t'atone for sin Jemmy must go with Terrapin...." Jemmy—President James Madison—was Vice-President under Jefferson when that administration introduced the hated embargo laws. Madison suffered from the country's hostility toward Jefferson's embargo policy even after the laws were repealed. The terrapin, the Federalist symbol of government oppression and specifically the Embargo, has President Madison still tightly in its grasp, even though he has cut off its head.

This cartoon, along with a verse entitled "The Death of the Embargo," written by William Cullen Bryant in 1808, was printed in *The New York Evening Post*. The engraving was originally designed by the leading portraitist and miniature painter John Welsey Jarvis, who was a close friend and admirer of Tom Paine and sculpted a fine bust of the American revolutionary writer. The cartoon itself was engraved by Dr. Alexander Anderson from Jarvis' design. Anderson was originally trained as a physician, but gave up the practice of medicine to devote his life to the graphic arts. He was greatly inspired by the work of Thomas Benwick, who had discovered the art of wood engraving in England at the end of the eighteenth century. And it was Anderson who introduced the art of wood engraving to the United States. He lived into his eighties and produced some 6,000 wood engravings.   G.B.

To the Grave Go Sham Protectors of "Free Trade and Sailors' Rights" — and All the People Say Amen!

"TO THE GRAVE GO SHAM PROTECTORS OF "FREE TRADE AND SAILORS' RIGHTS"—AND ALL THE PEOPLE SAY AMEN"

TERRAPIN'S ADDRESS.

Reflect, my friend, as you pass by ;
As you are, now, so, once, was I ;
As I am now, so you may be :—
Laid on your back to die like me !
I was, indeed, true Sailor born ;
To quit my friend, in death, I scorn.
Once Jemmy seem'd to be my friend,
But, basely, brought me to my end !
Of head bereft, and light, and breath,
I hold *Fidelity*, in death :—
For "*Sailor's Rights*" I still will tug :
And, Madison to death I'll hug,
For his perfidious zeal display'd,
For "*Sailor's Rights and for Free Trade*."
This small atonement I will have—
I'll hug down Jemmy to the grave.
Then Trade and Commerce shall be free
And Sailors have their liberty—
Of head bereft, and light, and breath,
The *Terrapin*, still true in death,
Still punish Jemmy's perfidy ;
Free Trade, and brave Sailors Free !

PASSENGERS REPLY.

Yes Terrapin, bereft of breath,
We see thee faithful still, in death :
Stick to't—"*Free Trade and Sailor's Right* :
Hug Jemmy—press him—hold him—bite—
Ne'er mind thy head—thou'lt live without it,
Spunk will preserve thy life—don't doubt it—
Down to the grave t'atone for sin,
Jemmy must go, with Terrapin.
Bear *him* but off, and we shall see
Commerce restor'd and Sailors Free !
Hug, Terrapin, with all thy might,
Now for "*Free Trade* and *Sailor's Right* :"
Stick to him, Terrapin, to thee the nation
Now eager looks :—then die for her salvation.

FLOREAT RESPUBLICA.

Banks of Goose Creek,
City of Washington,
15th April 1814.

FORD COLLECTION.

David Claypoole Johnston. "A Foot Race."
(1824). Etching. 8⅝ × 11½". Collection
American Antiquarian Society.

*

In one of the few campaign cartoons on the
early Presidency, David Claypoole Johnston
suggests the competitive nature of politics
through his creative device of the race and
the details of the cheering crowd. On the
left is a man waving a stovepipe hat, a figure symbolic of western support. There are
well-dressed men suggestive of wealthy citizens and ragged men representative of the
masses. Encouraging John Adams is the
image of New England, while the black
children typify the South.

With four strong leaders entered in the con-
test, all Democratic-Republicans, no one
candidate received the required majority of
the Electoral College votes nor an equal
measure of the popular ballots. Andrew
Jackson placed first with a plurality, John
Quincy Adams was second, William
Crawford finished third and Henry Clay
last. This situation forced the election into
the House of Representatives for the second
time in history, which resulted in Adams'
victory.

In the manner of many early nineteenth-
century cartoons, the literary element of
the picture takes up almost half of the
print.   G.B.

A FOOT RACE

A FOOT-RACE

1829-1861

Andrew Jackson to James Buchanan

David Claypoole Johnston. "Richard III". (1828). Engraving and stipple. 8½ × 5¹²⁄₁₆". Collection Boston Public Library, Print Department.

*

By the time of his election to the Presidency, Andrew Jackson had achieved the status of national hero on the basis of his military triumphs. At the same time, however, there existed another aspect of his national reputation as an exceptional battlefield strategist—and one that was repeatedly mentioned by both his personal and political enemies. For besides being acclaimed "Old Hickory," stalwart commander of America's frontier armies, Andrew Jackson was widely considered a ruthless, cold-blooded killer.

There were grounds for such sentiments, as the General had been a harsh and demanding military commander. In 1814 he had ordered the execution of four soldiers allegedly charged with desertion; and it was this order which returned to haunt Jackson in the 1828 campaign in the form of vituperative attacks mounted by Republican editors.

Perhaps the most original of these savage caricatures is David Claypoole Johnston's "Richard III," in which Jackson is adorned with a military hat topped with a smoke-belching cannon as its plume. His face and epaulets are fashioned out of naked figures representing those whose deaths can be attributed to Jackson's violent temper. Below stands a soup bowl whose ingredients are:

> Helpless orphans pitious cries,
> Scalding tears from widows eyes,
> Cool'd with tyrants daintiest food,
> Murder'd soldiers clotted blood.

Repeating the words of Shakespeare's Richard III, Jackson remarks that "the souls of all I had murder'd came to my tent."   D.E.

Methought the souls of all that I had murder'd, came to my tent. Act 5 Sc 3.

RICHARD III.

Edward Williams Clay. "The Rats Leaving a Falling House". 1831. Lithograph. 18¼ × 11¾". Collection American Antiquarian Society.

*

This cartoon deals with the resignation in 1831 of Andrew Jackson's cabinet. Four of its members—Berrien, Branch, Van Buren, and Barry—are depicted as scurrying rats fleeing the destruction of the President's "Altar of Reform" which, along with a column labelled "Public confidence in the stability and harmony of this administration," tumbles to the ground. Resignations rain down upon a bewildered Jackson, whose outstretched foot has found the tail of Secretary of State Van Buren, preventing his panicked flight.

This chaotic situation occurred when political rivalry became entwined with a petty status struggle in social Washington. The affair began as a dispute among the wives of the President's cabinet over Peggy Eaton, wife of the Secretary of War, Major John H. Eaton. Her rumored notorious past provoked a scandal among the more puritanical cabinet members and their wives, and they began to publicly ignore her. It is probable, however, that the real instigator was the ambitious senator from South Carolina, John C. Calhoun, who desired to rid the cabinet of those who stood as obstacles in his road to the White House. In an effort designed to drive her husband out of the cabinet, Calhoun and his allies took advantage of Mrs. Eaton's precarious social position, and succeeded in blowing the incident out of all proportion.

But Calhoun's plan backfired because Jackson, who felt that a similar attack had hastened his own wife's death in 1828, placed his sympathies with the Eatons. His chivalrous intervention failed to quiet the tempest. Jackson's solution was to accept the resignation of the cabinet. Only Van Buren, his Secretary of State and political confidant, stayed close to him. Calhoun was further alienated.

A highly gifted and unconventional caricaturist, Edward Williams Clay was, from 1829 until his death in 1857, one of the most inventive political cartoonists in America. "The Rats Leaving a Falling House" was one of the artist's most effective satires; it was widely circulated at the time and elicited much public comment. Perhaps the cartoon's extensive popularity can best be measured by this comment from Van Buren's son John. When asked when his father would be returning home from Washington, the young man replied, "When the President takes off his foot."   D.E.

THE RATS LEAVING A FALLING HOUSE

The Rats leaving a Falling House.

Artist Unknown. "King Andrew the First".
(1832). Lithograph. 12⅝ × 8⅝". Collection
Library of Congress.

*

To many Americans, Andrew Jackson was
a savior: a defender of the common man
and a vigorous attacker of privilege and
vested interest. But to as many others, and
particularly to the aristocratic statesmen
whose power he had usurped, Jackson was
not only an ignorant backwoods lout, he
was a dictatorial tyrant—a destroyer of
American liberties and an unwelcome inter-
loper in the political arena.

These divergent attitudes, combined with
a growing sophistication in lithographic
and printing techniques during the 1830s,
provoked a remarkable number of cartoons
which either extravagantly praised Jackson
or savagely attacked him.

One of the best of the opposition cartoons,
and one superior in its draftsmanship and
print quality, "King Andrew the First"
stands out as one of the most direct and
finest examples of political caricature ever
produced in the United States. Dressed in
the accoutrements of the despised and deca-
dent European royalty, Jackson deliberately
tramples on the Constitution, a ledger of
federal court decisions, and the American
watchwords of "Virtue, Liberty and Independence." It is a comment not only upon
Jackson's autocratic methods, but upon the
extent to which federal authority came to
be represented in the office of the President.
D.E.

BORN TO COMMAND.

OF VETO MEMORY.

HAD I BEEN CONSULTED.

KING ANDREW THE FIRST.

"A.H." "General Jackson Slaying the Many Headed Monster". (1836). Lithograph. 13½ × 16⅜". Collection Library of Congress. Published by H. R. Robinson, 1836.

*

The most controversial issue to emerge during Jackson's administration revolved around the re-chartering of the Second Bank of the United States. Though termed a "National Bank," it was in reality a privately controlled corporation "possessing unique and profitable relations with the government."[1] For not only was the bank exempt from all taxation and interest payments on public funds, but Congress had also given it a virtual monopoly over the nation's currency and credit.

Jackson had early voiced his objections to such a banking system, claiming that it was unconstitutional, un-democratic, and un-American for any corporation to possess such extensive economic powers. Aware of Jackson's views, Bank President Nicholas Biddle began to loosen credit restrictions on congressmen and newspaper editors in an effort to build support for the Bank's charter, due for renewal in 1836. However, Senators Henry Clay and Daniel Webster persuaded Biddle to press for re-chartering before the election of 1832, feeling that if the Charter passed in Congress, Jackson would be forced to either sign a bill he disliked, or veto an assumedly popular measure. Either way, the President would be politically embarrassed, and Clay, hopeful of national election, would benefit.

When the charter passed, Jackson, feeling personally attacked, "declared war to the death against the Bank and pushed it with all the energy and fury, in the same cut-and-thrust style that he had the war against the Indians and English twenty years before."[2]

One of many pro-Jackson cartoons was "Jackson Slaying the Many Headed Monster," in which the President, armed with his ever-present cane (here labelled "Veto"), strikes out at the Hydra-like Bank. The demon's largest head is that of Biddle himself, adorned with a hat inscribed "PENN... $35,000,000", signifying the Bank's home office in Philadelphia and the amount of its assets. The other heads, each possessing the name of a different state, represent the Bank's "four and twenty hideous" branches. Assisting are Vice-President Van Buren, and an odd-looking character named Major Jack Downing, a popular fictional hero who frequently accompanied Jackson in both literature and caricature, generally lending a helping hand, and often dispensing a likeable brand of homespun wit and insight.
D.E.

Notes
1. Arthur M. Schlesinger, Jr., *The Age of Jackson* (Boston, 1945), p. 74.
2. Michael Chevalier, *Society, Manners and Politics in the United States* (New York, 1961), p. 30.

GENERAL JACKSON SLAYING THE MANY HEADED MONSTER.

Artist Unknown. "Fifty Cents Shin Plaster". 1837. Lithograph. 12⅜ × 19¼". Collection Library of Congress. Published by H. R. Robinson, 1837.

*

When President Jackson, emphasizing the political power of the President, dealt the United States Bank its fatal blow by withdrawing the government's deposits, he set in motion a chain of events which led to the economic crash of 1837. At the time, most state banks were unreliable operations, far less carefully managed than was the centralized bank. Immediately upon receipt of federal monies, these banks began to issue large quantities of bills frequently backed with non-existent capital. As the monetary supply increased, wild speculation grew throughout the country, particularly in the West where land had become the most sought-after commodity. Western lands were purchased from the government either by would-be settlers or voracious speculators and federal revenues from those sales increased six-fold between 1834 and 1837. The government deposited approximately twenty-eight million dollars of this surplus in various state banks, which in turn loaned it out to speculators eager to buy more Western lands. Again the federal treasury received money from the sales and re-deposited it in the state banks, from which the speculators borrowed it to purchase still more land.

As time went on, it became increasingly evident that payments were being made with very flimsy currency. In an effort to halt this cycle, curtail rampant speculation, and avert large losses on the government's deposits, Jackson issued the "Specie Circular," which declared that the treasury would not accept paper money for land sales after August 15, 1836. After that date, all public lands could be paid for only in gold and silver. This created a demand for specie which most banks simply could not supply. These banks were forced to refuse redemption of their notes and many closed their doors. On May 10, 1837, they suspended all further specie payments.

The suspension led to the issuance by a number of cities, corporations, and even individuals, of small denominational paper notes derisively named "shinplasters." Many of these bills were elaborately decorated but were usually worthless. New York publisher H. R. Robinson responded by printing two lithographs which parodied these shinplasters (see no. 15, also).

"Fifty Cents Shin Plaster" depicts Jackson astride a pig followed by his Congressional ally, Thomas Hart Benton. Both furiously chase the "Gold Humbug" over the edge of a cliff. Steering the safer course is Van Buren, riding a fox and declaring that "although I follow in the footsteps of Jackson, it is expedient at this time to deviate a little." This was in reference both to the new President's political acumen as well as to his advocacy of an independent "Sub-Treasury" system designed to replace the National Bank. D.E.

FIFTY CENTS SHIN PLASTER

Napoleon Sarony. "Treasury Note 75
Cents". (1837). Lithograph. 11¾ × 19¼".
Collection Library of Congress. Published
by H. R. Robinson, 1837.

*

This lithograph was drawn by the talented
Napoleon Sarony, who was barely sixteen
years old in 1837. He portrayed recently-
inaugurated President Martin Van Buren
as a dragon atop a cart labelled "Treasury
Department." The vehicle, driven by the
President's son John, and drawn by men
with asses' ears, crushes a group of men
beneath its wheels. In the left panel, a dejected Jackson garbed in Columbia's costume sadly utters, "More Glory." Opposite,
he appears as an ass reciting his favorite
epithet, "By the Eternal!" On his back,
Jackson carries a sack of gold coins, popu-
larly referred to as "Mint Drops." Van
Buren follows, remarking, "Glory Enough,"
as he catches Jackson's excretions with his
hat.   D.E.

TREASURY NOTE 75 CENTS

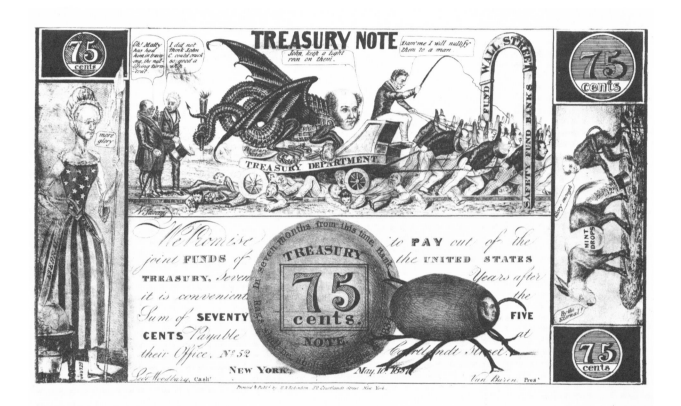

Edward Williams Clay. "All on Hobbies, Gee Up, Gee Ho!" 1838. Lithograph. 11¼ × 19". Collection Library of Congress. Published by H. R. Robinson, 1838.

*

America's leading statesmen during the Jacksonian Era are portrayed here, each riding his personal hobby. Leading is President Martin Van Buren, who in an effort to replace the United States Bank, advocated a sub-treasury system designed to separate Bank and State. His policies closely followed those of his predecessor; and as Jackson's hand-picked successor, Van Buren sits astride an "Old Hickory nag." Following is Senator Thomas Hart Benton of Missouri, the foremost supporter of Van Buren's fiscal policies. Known as "Old Bullion" for his hard money stance, Benton rides a "Golden Poney." Tandem on the third horse are Whig party Senators Henry Clay and Daniel Webster, leaders of Congressional opposition to Van Buren's financial programs. Next is John C. Calhoun on a horse labelled "State Rights and Nullification." The rider in military garb is General William Henry Harrison, who had unsuccessfully opposed Van Buren in 1836. He is seated on the "Anti-Masonic" steed, for he had been that party's candidate as well as the Whig nominee. Riding the "Abolition" hobby horse is former President John Quincy Adams, at the time of this cartoon a member of the House of Representatives. In 1836, Adams had asserted that slavery could be legally abolished through application of the federal government's war powers. However his "Ebony" steed does not appear to be faring well at all.

Drawn by E. W. Clay, the cartoon displays a significant lack of quick wit and comic exaggeration. Its humor lies completely in an extensive use of puns and familiar phrases, and indeed, it seems to have been designed to serve a dual purpose: to both satirize and instruct in the current political action. It works to such an extent that the cartoon transcends caricature and becomes a lesson on the politics of the day.   D.E.

ALL ON HOBBIES, GEE UP, GEE HO!

Artist Unknown. "Clar de Kitchen". (1840). Lithograph. 12⅜ × 17¼". Collection Library of Congress. Published by H. R. Robinson, 1840.

*

Named after a popular song of the period, this imaginative cartoon depicts newly-elected Whig President William Henry Harrison as an angry housewife driving the Democrats from her new (political) home. Although he appears a forceful man, Harrison, an Indian war hero, did not assert himself during the campaign. A Virginia-born aristocrat, he quietly watched while party leaders portrayed him as a humble man of the people. The Whigs wisely kept their candidate cloistered on his Ohio farm, while a committee, derisively called the "keepers of the General's conscience," handled his correspondence.[1] Harrison rarely appeared in public, and when he did he kept silent on the major issues, preferring instead to utter such platitudes as, "I believe and I say it is true Democratic feeling, that all the measures of the Government are directed to making the rich richer, and the poor poorer."[2]

After Harrison's overwhelming victory, the Democrats found themselves powerless for the first time in twelve years, and as the cartoon suggests they were quickly removed. The entire Democratic leadership is pictured fleeing from Harrison's wrath. John C. Calhoun declares "I am for the South direct," while Nicholas Biddle begs him to stay. Treasury Secretary Levi Woodbury laments that he can no longer issue Treasury notes. Joel R. Poinsett, Secretary of War, castigates Van Buren for not heeding his advice, and Vice-Presidential aspirant William Smith sadly reflects on his lost chance for glory. Also included are Democratic editor Francis P. Blair, and a dejected Amos Kendall, both long-time Jacksonians. But the most pitiful figure is Van Buren, who sadly notes that the current situation is "worse than the rebellion in Vermont," where he had been defeated by a humiliating margin of over 14,000 votes.

The identity of the cartoonist is unclear, but the pseudonym "Boneyshanks" was certainly taken from the well-known English cartoonist Cruickshank. It has been suggested, however, that "Clar de Kitchen" was drawn either by Napoleon Sarony or by David Claypoole Johnston, a controversial cartoonist who frequently signed his caricatures with nonsensical pen-names like "Crackfardi" and "Quiz."   D.E.

Notes
1. *Washington Globe*, April 13, 1840.
2. Arthur M. Schlesinger, Jr., *The Age of Jackson* (Boston, 1945), p. 292.

CLAR DE KITCHEN

Edward Williams Clay. "The Times". (1840). Lithograph. 13¼ × 19¼". Collection Library of Congress.

*

Andrew Jackson may have been justified in his fight against the United States Bank, but his abolition of the national bank was a major cause of the panic of 1837. Three years later, Philadelphia's Edward W. Clay, a very versatile artist, drew an elaborate cartoon illustrating the severe economic troubles. Clay's lithograph, "The Times," had the panoramic elaboration and the broad social comment of William Hogarth, the great master of narrative realism, whose impact on the art of popular imagery was still strong a century after he had made most of his master engravings.

In the center of the cartoon we see a run on the Mechanics Bank. In the foreground workers idly stand around, some with bare feet, while the family on the left is becoming inebriated on gin. In addition to the sin of drunkeness we are also presented with usury, as posters advertise money lent at 7% a month. Next to this attractive offer there is an announcement of a "Grand Scheme," evidently a lottery, while the sheriff on the right auctions off foreclosed property. Everything is bad: the Street Hotel is for sale, the factory is closed, idle ships are tied up on the river in the background. Only the liquor store and the pawnbroker are doing business on the "61st Anniversary of Our Independence." High in the sky above all this misery, a white silk hat and the famous "glory spectacles" symbolize President Andrew Jackson.

Above a notice advertising good prices for old rags (on the fence in the foreground), H. R. Robinson has also managed to advertise his printing shop for "Caricatures... Courtland Street." Robinson was the publisher of this broadsheet which conveys an anti-Jacksonian message with comic boldness.   P.S.

THE TIMES.

Edward Williams Clay. "Polk's Dream". (1846). Lithograph. 12⅞ × 17". Collection Library of Congress. Published by James Baille, April 1846.

*

Shortly after his election in 1844, James Knox Polk outlined his major political objectives to newly-appointed Secretary of the Navy, George Bancroft. "There are four measures," he declared, "which are to be the measures of my administration: one, a reduction of the tariff; another, the independent treasury; a third, the settlement of the Oregon question; and lastly, the acquisition of California."[1] By quickly moving forward with a quiet determination and a strong executive will unencumbered by personal ambition, Polk realized each of these goals well before the end of his administration.

Published just two months before the agreement with the British that was to bring the Oregon territories under American jurisdiction, "Polk's Dream," a cluttered, yet subtle and imaginative cartoon by E. W. Clay, stresses the President's commitment to the policies of Manifest Destiny and his obsession with the Oregon crisis. Polk is confronted by a demonic apparition which hides behind the mask of his hero and political mentor, Andrew Jackson, demanding:

> Child of my adoption, on whom my mantle hath fallen, swear never to take your toe off that line should you deluge your country with seas of blood, produce a servile insurrection and dislocate every joint of this happy and prosperous union!

Polk, foot on the 54° 40' line on the Oregon map, vows to obey the command with a Jacksonian, "By the Eternal." On his bed-table lay four books: *The Art of War*, a thesis entitled *Practical Piety*, *Calvin's Works*, and a biography of Napoleon—all of which indicate the ideas with which the President had of late been occupied. Three cabinet members, alarmed by the noise of Polk's nightmare, rush to his bedside. At the extreme left is ardent expansionist Bancroft. Ahead of him strides Secretary of State James Buchanan, who, brandishing a packet of letters from British Ambassador Richard Packenham, detects a strong smell of brimstone but is characteristically unable to perceive its source. Also pictured is Treasury Secretary Robert James Walker, who carries the new tariff bill under his arm while declaring the President a patriot even in his dreams.   D.E.

Note

1. James Schouler, *A History of the United States of America Under the Constitution* (New York, 1894-1913), Vol. IV, p. 498.

POLK'S DREAM.

"Peter Smith". "Knock'd into a Cock'd Hat". (1848). Lithograph. 14 × 21¾". Collection Library of Congress.

*

Zachary Taylor's glaring lack of qualifications for the Presidency, combined with his unwillingness—or inability—to answer questions of policy, inspired few favorable cartoons during the election of 1848. One of the rare pro-Whig cartoons produced was "Knock'd Into a Cock'd Hat," which forecast a Taylor victory. A cannonball, upon which the General's face is imprinted, has been fired from a cannon labelled "Philadelphia Convention," upsetting the Democratic nominee, Lewis Cass.

The 1848 campaign was a particularly divisive one. Sectional differences, fueled by the slavery controversy, created splits in both major parties. The Whigs themselves issued no platform, so diverse were the views within their ranks. The Democrats were even less cohesive. The party's New York members had divided into two factions: the conservative "Hunkers," (so-called because they hunkered for office), and the anti-slavery "Barnburners," their name taken from the popular tale of a Dutch farmer who believed that the best way to rid his barn of rats was to burn it to the ground. Both groups sent full delegations to the Baltimore convention, but when a compromise decision allowed each delegate only half a vote, the Barnburners angrily stalked out and the Hunkers refused to vote at all.

The two parties faced a great challenge from a group of anti-slavery Whigs, Liberty party members and Barnburners who nominated Van Buren for the Presidency. They drew up a strong anti-slavery platform and took as their slogan, "Free soil, free speech, free labor, free men." These "Free-soilers" succeeded in splitting the Democratic vote between Cass and Van Buren, leaving Taylor victorious. While Taylor, an undistinguished President, was a "minority" choice, the same can be said of distinguished Presidents such as Abraham Lincoln and Woodrow Wilson. D.E.

KNOCK'D INTO A COCK'D HAT.

Artist Unknown. "An Available Candidate: The One Qualification for a Whig President". (1848). Lithograph. 17⅝ × 12⅛". Collection Library of Congress. Published by Nathaniel Currier, 1848.

*

As the title of this excellent cartoon suggests, General Zachary Taylor became the Whig nominee in 1848 because he was the party's most "available candidate." As the election rapidly approached, Whig leaders, desperate for a political victory, narrowed the field to three likely prospects: Senators Henry Clay and Daniel Webster, and Mexican War hero Zachary Taylor. But as Clay and Webster both held strong anti-slavery views, their Presidential appeal was hardly universal. Realizing that they needed a man who could satisfy both Northern and Southern voters, the Whigs deemed a military man the most promising choice. A number of factors led to Zachary Taylor. First and foremost, he was a war hero. His victory at Buena Vista had been a decisive battle in the recent Mexican War, and had earned him the popular nickname, "Old Rough and Ready." Furthermore, Taylor's Southern birth, his ownership of some three hundred slaves, and his clean political record (so clean that in fact he had never voted), all pointed to him as the most desirable candidate.

For most Whigs the nomination of a war hero was a radical turnabout. A majority has opposed the war from its outset, feeling that hostilities had been instigated by Polk and his Southern friends for the sole purpose of extending slavery to newly conquered territories. Thus the hypocritical choice of a war hero did not go unnoticed. The Democrats knew that Taylor had been nominated for purely practical reasons, and this realization provoked both a large editorial response and many satirical cartoons.

"An Available Candidate" is one of the best of these caricatures. It depicts a smug, warrior-like Taylor enthroned upon a pyramid of skulls—grisly symbols of the means by which the General had achieved his fame. The cartoon is thus unlike any previous American political caricature, for while earlier efforts had frequently been vicious in their attacks, never before had one been so scathing in such stunningly visual terms. "An Available Candidate" demonstrated that no words were needed when the quality of illustration reached this level of excellence.   D.E.

AN AVAILABLE CANDIDATE: THE ONE QUALIFICATION FOR A WHIG PRESIDENT

AN AVAILABLE CANDIDATE.
THE ONE QUALIFICATION FOR A WHIG PRESIDENT.

Artist Unknown. "Position of the Democratic Party in 1852". (1852). Lithograph. 14 × 20". Collection Library of Congress.

*

The nomination in 1852 of Franklin Pierce as Presidential candidate satisfied most Democrats, for he was a likeable, well-mannered man who had not been in politics long enough to make many enemies or to make his principles known to the voters. He had both Northern and Southern support, and since he was only forty-eight, he also appealed to the party's "Young Americans"— a group of youthful, hot-blooded firebrands who were rapidly gaining control of the party. These factors, combined with his Mexican War service, his pliable personality, and his blameless political record, made Franklin Pierce ideal Presidential material.

The platform upon which Pierce ran was consistent with previous Democratic planks. Through it the party upheld the Compromise of 1850, vowing to faithfully execute all of its provisions including the controversial Fugitive Slave Law. This stance came under scathing attack from Republicans and Free-Soilers. Both groups objected to the Democrats' pro-slavery posture and to the "doughfaced" attitude of their candidate. To them, Pierce was merely a Southerner in disguise; a Northerner whose political views belonged south of the Mason-Dixon line.

This feeling is graphically expressed in the "Position of the Democratic Party in 1852," an inexpertly drawn if not child-like rendering—yet one which effectively presented the case against Pierce. The "slavocratic" candidate kneels at the feet of a slaveholder who commands him to grovel over "Mason & Dixon's Line" to which the Democratic Baltimore platform constructed out of "Southern Pine" is attached. Pierce gladly acquieces as the Spirit of Jefferson bemoans his "degenerate Sons." As the Devil applauds, his "servants," defeated Presidential hopefuls Cass and Douglas, sadly agree that Pierce has "outhunkered" even them. The remaining figure, Baron Julius von Haynau, was a Hungarian general whose cruel deeds had become infamous the world over. He wears a Brewer's pot on his head, for he had been assaulted by the workers of Barclay's Brewery while in England. The notorious Baron declares that he feels "quite at home" among the Democrats of America. D.E.

POSITION OF THE DEMOCRATIC PARTY IN 1852

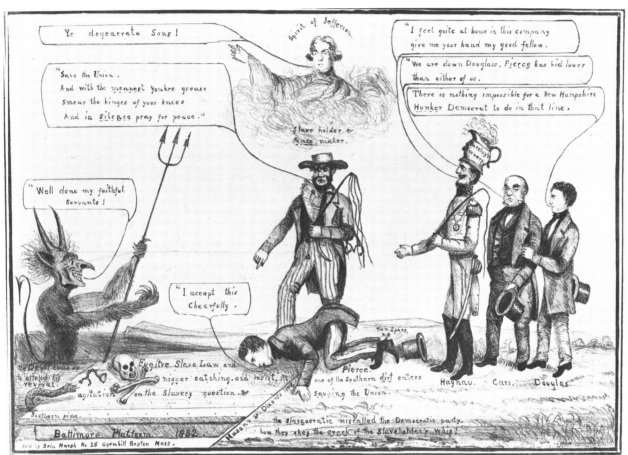

Position of the Democratic Party in 1852.
"Freemen of America, how long will you be led by such Leaders!"

Michael Angelo Woolf. "Our National Bird as it Appeared When Handed to James Buchanan. March 4, 1857 / The Identical Bird as it Appeared A.D. 1861". (1861). Lithograph. 7⅝ × 13". Collection Boston Public Library, Print Department. Published by Thomas W. Strong, 1861.

*

Published at the moment of President James Buchanan's retirement, this lithograph presents a savage indictment of the President's ineffective actions during the growing sectional crisis. Upon Buchanan's inauguration the American eagle, symbol of a strong Union, had stood vigorous and defiant; four years later it appears broken and dejected, shorn of its once proud feathers and sharp talons. Standing on two wooden stumps labelled "Anarchy" and "Secession," the helpless bird blames its pitiful transformation on the outgoing administration with the Shakespearean line, "I was murdered i' the capitol."

When Buchanan left the Presidency in March 1861, Southern representatives had already withdrawn from Congress, and the Confederacy had been declared. The President's conciliatory policies, combined with his unwillingness to pursue a forceful course and his desire to postpone the crisis until he was safely out of office, had not brought an end to regional differences. Instead, Buchanan had lost the confidence of the North while the South was left embittered, antagonized, and preparing for war.

While the cartoon is unusual in that no human figures are represented, the "National Bird" was by no means a rare figure in cartoons of the period. The American eagle had appeared at Columbia's side in "Little Bo Peep and her Foolish Sheep" by Thomas W. Strong while a Union cartoon published in 1862 depicted the plucking of the Confederate Crow. But the most noteworthy example was "Plucked," which appeared in 1846. It portrayed the Mexican eagle in exactly the same fashion as "Our National Bird"; for it showed a strong, healthy bird — symbol of a powerful nation — reduced to a weak and defenseless shadow of its former self.   D.E.

OUR NATIONAL BIRD AS IT APPEARED WHEN HANDED TO JAMES BUCHANAN. MARCH 4, 1857 /
THE IDENTICAL BIRD AS IT APPEARED A.D. 1861

OUR NATIONAL BIRD AS IT APPEARED WHEN HANDED TO JAMES BUCHANAN. MARCH. 4. 1857.

THE IDENTICAL BIRD AS IT APPEARED .A .D. 1861.

"I was murdered i' the Capitol"

Shakespere

Henry Louis Stephans. "Proposed Meeting of Ex-Presidents". (1861). Wood engraving. Plate dimensions, 9¾ × 7⅛". Collection The General Library, University of California, Berkeley. Appeared in *Vanity Fair*, May 11, 1861.

*

While many professional humorists were active during the decade prior to the Civil War, very few of their works were included in those magazines exclusively devoted to satire. For during that time newspapers and periodicals of all kinds amply supplied the demand for printed humor through their regular comic columns. Consequently, of the fourteen comic periodicals published during the 1850s, only two survived for any appreciable length of time. The longest-lived was *Yankee Notions*, which ran for fifteen years from 1852 to 1867. Yet perhaps the best was *Vanity Fair*, whose premier issue appeared on December 31, 1859.

Admittedly an imitation of the London *Punch* in both size and appearance, *Vanity Fair* vowed to deal harshly with "political tricksters, venal editors, public charlatans, silly authors, and all people whose stupidity necessitates their being treated as criminals."[1] But another reason for both the contemporary success and enduring historical value of *Vanity Fair*, was the quality of its cartoons. Largely the work of Henry Louis Stephans—who, until the appearance of Thomas Nast in 1861, produced the period's most striking and original graphic humor— the magazine's political cartoons formed an integral part of *Vanity Fair's* comic format.

One of the finest examples of Stephans' work was the "Proposed Meeting of Ex-Presidents." It lampooned a suggestion to bring the five living ex-Presidents together for the purpose of formulating a possible solution to the secession crisis. Dressed as a haggling group of spinsters, the former chief executives reveal exactly how such an unprecedented gathering could easily degenerate into a heated argument concerning responsibility for the crisis. Rather than attempting to deny that their actions helped intensify the regional conflicts, however, Stephans depicts the five men trying to outdo each other in claiming the most credit for the disruption of the Union.   D.E.

Note
1. *Vanity Fair*, Vol. I, no. 1, preface, p. 1.

VANITY FAIR.

PROPOSED MEETING OF EX-PRESIDENTS.

VAN BUREN.—"I THINK I SHOULD PRESIDE AT THIS MEETING, FOR I LAID THE FOUNDATION OF THIS TREASON BY SPLITTING THE DEMOCRATIC PARTY ON THE BUFFALO PLATFORM."

PIERCE.—"I THINK I DESERVE ESPECIAL CONSIDERATION, FOR I PUT JEFF DAVIS IN MY CABINET AS SECRETARY OF WAR, AFTER HE HAD BEEN RE-JECTED BY THE PEOPLE OF MISSISSIPPI FOR HIS DISUNION SENTIMENTS."

BUCHANAN.—"GOD KNOWS I SHOULD HAVE PRECEDENCE, FOR WITH FLOYD AND THE REST OF MY CABINET I BROUGHT ABOUT THE PRESENT REBELLION."

JOHN TYLER.—"I DESERVE THE FIRST PLACE, FOR I AM IDENTIFIED WITH THE TRAITORS AS OPENLY WORKING FOR THE DISRUPTION OF THE UNION."

FILLMORE.—"AS POSITIVE COUNCILS ARE NOW ONLY AVAILABLE, AND AS I AM NOT IN THAT LINE, I'LL LEAVE."

1861-1869

Abraham Lincoln to Andrew Johnson

Adalbert John Volck. "Passage Through Baltimore". (1863). Etching. 7⁹⁄₁₆ × 4⁵⁄₃₂". Collection Maryland Historical Society.

*

In "Passage Through Baltimore" cartoonist Adalbert Volck made his first and funniest attack on Abraham Lincoln. In his tam-o-shanter, the terrified new President peers from a Philadelphia, Wilmington and Baltimore Railroad Co. boxcar containing "Bones" (perhaps a reference to a musical instrument associated with slaves). He is totally intimidated by a hissing cat.

According to rumor, Lincoln feared assassination in Baltimore and had been spirited through to Washington for his inauguration disguised as a Scotsman. While the story of his disguise was a fabrication, the cartoon did reflect the pitiful condition of the Presidency. Having no government agents to protect him, Lincoln was forced to rely on private detectives and secret trains. His prestige was so low that the possibility that he might be mobbed was very real. He had been elected by regional minority, and without the participation of the South in the election. Thus, to say the least, his popularity in Maryland was minimal. Indeed, that people would believe the Scotsman tale demonstrated in how much contempt they held the office—or at least its new occupant.

This plate is the second in a series most commonly known as the *Confederate War Etchings*. It appeared in the first issue, known as *Sketches from the Civil War in North America*. Because of the explosive situation in Maryland immediately after the outbreak of the war, and because of that state's importance to the Union, Volck's powerful drawings which were friendly to

the Confederate cause had been suppressed by the federal government as early as 1861, when only ten of them had been issued. After their suppression, Volck produced the rest in secret and distributed them under a false London imprint to "subscribers" only. He signed them with the anagram "V. Blada," part of his own name spelled backwards.

Volck's technique of using a line drawing of high contrast is most effective here. The composition is bold and the impression instant. He has succeeded, without a word of caption, in conveying his view of a Lincoln devoid of courage or dignity.   M.S.

PASSAGE THROUGH BALTIMORE

Adalbert John Volck. "Don Quixote and Sancho Panza". (c. 1868). Etching. 5%₃₂ × 6%₃₂". Collection Maryland Historical Society.

*

In this etching Lincoln plays Don Quixote to General Benjamin Butler's Sancho Panza. The cartoon reflects the feeling that Butler, a man who symbolized cruelty and greed to the South, had an unwarranted degree of influence over President Lincoln. However effective, Volck's satire missed the point. Butler was only one of many officers; he was not Lincoln's right-hand man. After much experience with ambitious and unsuccessful generals, the President eventually chose better men to lead his armies: Ulysses S. Grant, William T. Sherman, George H. Thomas. In making his choices, Lincoln exerted powers over military strategy and general control of the war which no chief executive before him had so much needed to do. In the face of active Congressional attempts to control the war, it was the President who set the pace and determined policy. Although legislators acted with rare vigor, they never managed to regain the initiative.

In "Don Quixote and Sancho Panza" Volck displays his very sophisticated mastery of line, a surprising ability in view of his relatively limited art training. He uses a broken, scratchy line which reinforces the sense of vagueness and purposelessness which these two figures project. They seem to be wandering aimlessly in the desert, knowing neither where they are going nor why.
C.B./M.S.

DON QUIXOTE AND SANCHO PANZA

Sir John Tenniel. "Abe Lincoln's Last Card; or, Rouge-Et-Noir". (1862). Wood engraving. Plate dimensions, 7⅜ × 9¾". Collection The General Library, University of California, Berkeley. Appeared in *Punch*, October 18, 1862.

*

In "Abe Lincoln's Last Card," Sir John Tenniel gave Punch a sardonic version of President Lincoln's emancipation of the slaves in the rebel states. Desperate for victory, the President throws down a spade while the Southerner holds the winning card and smiles in anticipation of victory. If President Lincoln acted from any motive other than military necessity, Tenniel does not show it.

To some extent, Tenniel was right. Lincoln did not emancipate the slaves simply because of his hatred for slavery, but because of his commitment to the Union. There were many complicated reasons involved: to give the cause a moral tinge in the eyes of the world and thus prevent foreign recognition of the Confederacy; to cripple the Confederacy by depriving it of its labor supply; to satisfy radical Republicans; and to encourage hitherto rebellious slave states to declare for the Union before the measure went into effect in January, 1863. All of these reasons helped to explain the Emancipation Proclamation.

Yet equally important was the fact that in the states which had seceded, the President —not the Congress—brought about freedom to the slaves, and with little or no Constitutional sanction. At that time, in *fact*, the power to regulate slavery belonged to the states. But in time of crisis, so great were Presidential powers that they extended into areas which in peace time were closed to all three branches of the federal government. By his proclamation, Lincoln made himself the moral spokesman of his party and of the Union cause, and the single most important figure in suppressing the rebellion.

Like Matt Morgan, Tenniel had a distaste for Lincoln and the North which mellowed only near the close of the war. It is not surprising then, to see his version of the American President as an awkward, indignant, desperate man. He shows Lincoln's long legs all asprawl, as though even these are too much for the man to handle. His hair—drawn up to resemble devil's horns—and his protruding jaw, combine to give him an air of ferocity without real power. The contrast with the more graceful profile of the Southerner tells us instantly who Tenniel believes to be the cleverest of the two, and the more likely to succeed.

Born in London in 1820, Sir John Tenniel was a well-known English book illustrator, as well as a cartoonist for *Punch* magazine. He spent a short time at the Royal Academy but soon passed from painting in oils and watercolors into illustration; perhaps his most famous work in this respect is Lewis Carroll's *Alice in Wonderland*.   C.B./M.S.

ABE LINCOLN'S LAST CARD; OR, ROUGE-ET-NOIR

PUNCH, OR THE LONDON CHARIVARI.— OCTOBER 18, 1862.

ABE LINCOLN'S LAST CARD; OR, ROUGE-ET-NOIR.

Thomas Nast. "Compromise with the South". (1864). Wood engraving. Plate dimensions, 9¼ × 13⅞". Collection The General Library, University of California, Berkeley. Appeared in *Harper's Weekly*, September 3, 1864.

*

In his woodcut, "Compromise with the South," Thomas Nast showed readers of *Harper's Weekly* what anything but unconditional surrender by the South would mean. In this one cartoon, Nast captured the moral fervor of the Union cause, and the Northern view of Davis. Since Northerners saw secession as illegal, they felt that the Confederate levying of war on the federal government was rank treason. Davis was chief traitor, a defender of outrageous murders and slavery, who deserved all the blame for the war and enough hemp to fit him on the gallows.

One of Nast's first cartoons for *Harper's Weekly*, "Compromise with the South" was, however, not the first example of his use of art to editorialize. For two years he had done just that in illustrations and large allegorical compositions, rich in patriotism and sentimentality. The subject of Jefferson Davis therefore suited Nast's pencil perfectly. Arrogant, sinister, the supreme rebel dominates the scene of carnage while Columbia and the Union soldier hide their faces in shame.

American political cartooning was ripe for an artist such as Nast. As weekly magazines such as *Harper's* gained popularity and provided a new medium for illustration, they summoned talent from everywhere; even Winslow Homer did pictures for the periodicals. Before Nast, no great cartoonist had gripped attention in America the way Honoré Daumier and John Leech had abroad. *Harper's Weekly* offered Nast a perfect forum, a limited Republican audience, and a method of printing cartoons by wood engraving that complemented his style. He offered his publishers popularity and new levels in comic art.   M.S.

COMPROMISE WITH THE SOUTH

Artist Unknown. "Running the 'Machine'". (1864). Lithograph. 13⅜ × 16⅞". Collection Library of Congress. Published by Currier and Ives, 1864.

*

This Democratic cartoon of 1864 holds both President Lincoln and his cabinet up for sharp derision. Lincoln appears as a joking buffoon; Secretary of War Edwin Stanton is an incompetent, accepting with joy the feeblest of victories; Secretary of the Navy Gideon Welles is shown as an addlepated dotard; Secretary of State William Seward is a blustering tyrant; and Secretary of the Treasury William P. Fessenden gloomily undermines the national credit with a flood of paper money.

But in truth, Lincoln had a powerful cabinet with many good men. Stanton and Welles worked hard and well; Seward had pliability and discretion; after Seward, Salmon P. Chase and Fessenden "ran the machine" efficiently. The President not only got the best out of his cabinet, he balanced each man's powers effectively so that no one man dominated the administration. Where some secretaries of state had acted as virtual prime ministers, Lincoln made himself the final source of foreign and domestic policy. In much the same way, the President was a virtuoso in dealing with party factions in Congress; he gave a little to both radicals and conservatives.

The style of this cartoon is not unlike the rather primitive style of American painters of the first half of the century. It was quite popular with the public, and reflects the relatively simple demands made upon art and wit by early nineteenth-century Americans. The humor in these cartoons resides not in the caricatures, but in the script, which is often lengthy and loaded with puns. This comparatively unsophisticated cartooning style not only dominated the first half of the century, it survived into the 1860s when it received competition from the more sophisticated graphic style and powerful wit of Thomas Nast.

Currier and Ives published cartoons which both favored and criticized President Lincoln. This policy was doubtless partially responsible for the firm reaching its peak of production during the 1850s and 1860s.

The precision with which the faces were rendered—in a portrait-like manner and without much exaggeration—points to the influence of early photography. C.B./M.S.

RUNNING THE "MACHINE".

Sir John Tenniel. "The Federal Phoenix". (1864). Wood engraving. Plate dimensions, 9¾ × 7¹⁄₁₆". Collection The General Library, University of California, Berkeley. Appeared in *Punch*, December 3, 1864.

*

In 1864, John Tenniel drew "The Federal Phoenix" for *Punch*, depicting a brutal Lincoln rising to glory from the fire that consumes the Bill of Rights and the Declaration of Independence. Bitter as it was, the cartoon echoed a legitimate "Copperhead" or anti-war Democratic complaint: in order to defend the Constitution, and the nation's laws, the President had transgressed on both. Lincoln did, in fact, order two newspapers suppressed for false information, and his generals destroyed several more. The military arrested men without warrants, held them without charges, and sentenced them without a jury trial. Troops arrested one enemy of the administration at his home and banished him to the Confederacy. Critics questioned the Constitutionality of the President calling for volunteers without Congressional approval, or drafting men into the army without Constitutional provision. Even staunch Unionist Democrats like Horatio Seymour of New York wondered aloud if love of liberty justified repression.

Sir John Tenniel (he was knighted in 1893) worked for *Punch* magazine for most of his life, and this cartoon is a good example of the graphic style he brought to that publication. Dry, linear, and immediate, he never sought the complex detail or somber halftones of Thomas Nast. Tenniel's work has the quality of illustration, for he was as much an illustrator as a cartoonist. Indeed, some have said he never achieved the extreme exaggeration of features that defines the true caricature. Tenniel's characters can always be easily identified: they have a certain portrait-like quality which a true caricaturist would avoid. In "The Federal Phoenix," however, Tenniel comes perhaps closer than anything he ever did to transforming his character into something entirely different from what he actually was. Tenniel assumed that his audience would understand the symbol of the phoenix, the ancient legendary bird said to consume itself in fire and then rise again from the ashes, refreshed and youthful; and he therefore gave no caption to his illustration. The reelected Lincoln soars upward, beard and hair drawn into bird-like beak and topknot, a look of malevolent determination on his face. In transforming Lincoln into something strange and inhuman, Tenniel has drawn one of his most vicious anti-Lincoln cartoons. M.S.

PUNCH, OR THE LONDON CHARIVARI.—December 3, 1864.

THE FEDERAL PHŒNIX.

Thomas Nast. ["Columbia Grieving at Lincoln's Bier"]. (1865). Woodcut. 16¾ × 23½". Collection Mr. and Mrs. Draper Hill, Memphis, Tennessee. Appeared in *Harper's Weekly*, April 29, 1865.

*

With malice toward none, with charity for all, with firmness in the right as God gives us to see the right, let us strive on to finish the work we are in, to bind up the nation's wounds, to care for him who shall have borne the battle and for his widow and his orphan, to do all which may achieve and cherish a just and lasting peace among ourselves and with all nations.

President Abraham Lincoln's Second Inaugural Address
4 March, 1865

COLUMBIA GRIEVING AT LINCOLN'S BIER

HARPER'S WEEKLY.

Thomas Nast. "Andrew Johnson's Reconstruction and How it Works". (1866). Wood engraving and letter press. Plate dimensions, 20¼ × 13⅝". Collection The General Library, University of California, Berkeley. Appeared in *Harper's Weekly*, September 1, 1866.

*

At the end of the Civil War, the problem of reuniting the nation was a delicate one demanding intelligent leadership. The Northern Congress agreed that before the South could return to Congress and to self-government, it must guarantee the civil rights of blacks, place loyal men in state government posts, uphold the federal war debt, and renounce secession. Southern leaders were willing to admit that they had lost, but unwilling to concede much more, and looked to the President for guidance and indications as to how much they must concede.

In October, 1866, Nast gave the readers of *Harper's Weekly* a savage indictment of Andrew Johnson's Reconstruction policy. Johnson was honest and well-meaning but not very effective. A Unionist Southern Democrat eager to forgive the returning rebels and not very interested in helping the freed slaves, he pardoned lavishly, set up new Southern governments without Congressional consent, allowed old enemies of the Union to return to power, and exacted few concessions from the South. When Congress interfered, he vetoed their bills to feed, clothe, and give civil rights to blacks, and accused the radical Republicans of plotting his murder. Unwilling to compromise, he forced a moderate Republican Congress to make policy without him. By July, 1866,

it had overruled his vetoes and virtually read him from the party; before it could do so, he tried unsuccessfully to found a party of his own.

Owing less to the grotesque style of Gillray than to the refined cross-hatched woodcuts of John Tenniel, Thomas Nast gave a new accuracy to the art of caricature in America. He also gave it a new feeling for culture, for in addition to his love of Shakespearean quotation, he alluded to well-known paintings and used them as models (e.g., the scene in the upper left-hand corner is reminiscent of Goya's *The Firing Squad, May 3, 1808*. He also quoted extensively from the statements of the men and newspapers he attacked, plastering their words on convenient walls in his cartoons to add to the force of his indictments. Another departure from traditional political cartooning was his ability to twist a face in order to make it both ridiculous and sinister without sacrificing recognition. His sketches of Johnson blend almost perfect likeness with a sense of narrow-minded malice, shown by the slightest turn of the mouth and hardness around the eyes.   M.S.

ANDREW JOHNSON'S RECONSTRUCTION AND HOW IT WORKS

Henry Louis Stephans. "A Fight for the Championship". (1868). Wood engraving. 15¾ × 11". Collection The University of Chicago Library. Appeared in *Frank Leslie's Illustrated Newspaper*, February 15, 1868.

*

Henry L. Stephans' woodcut of "A Fight for the Championship" in *Leslie's Weekly* treated a crisis of government with broad humor. The comics show President Johnson and Secretary of War Edwin Stanton squaring off (they disagreed about Reconstruction policy); Johnson discharging "his right hand and his Secretary" (Johnson suspended Stanton from office when he refused to resign); the Secretary striking back (the Senate ruled Johnson's suspension illegal under the Tenure of Office Act and restored Stanton); Johnson trying to settle the fight over General Grant's shoulder (Grant refused to act as a cat's-paw against the Secretary); and the probable outcome: mutual collapse. Benjamin Butler and Thaddeus Stevens, leading radical Republicans in the House, hold the Secretary up while the Secretary of State gives Johnson moral support.

Comic opera intrigue disguised a deadly serious issue. Distrusting the President, and sure that he would use his powers to hamstring implementation of their Reconstruction acts in the South, Congress had taken away his right to remove men from office without its approval, and had vested much of the military authority in General Grant. As Secretary of War, Stanton's post was vital to enforcement of military Reconstruction since the official who controlled the War Department controlled the army, and with it the process under which blacks and loyal whites would hold elections for conventions that would create new Southern governments. By firing Stanton and several of the subordinate generals, Johnson endangered the Congressional Republican Reconstruction policy.

On another level, however, the question was larger than this specific issue—it was one of Presidential power. How much influence in making policy should a President be allowed? Who should be commander of the army? How much right does a President have in the selection of his own advisers? Deprived of control over military and civil appointments and not allowed to make policy, the executive would become a mere figurehead. This Johnson would not permit, and in February, 1868 he ordered the removal of the Secretary of War despite the Congressional interdict.

Henry Stephans was an Englishman who had acted as art director for the short-lived humor magazine *Vanity Fair* until its demise in 1863. Employing a favorite cartoonist device of translating a political event into a sporting one, Stephans gave his caricature spirit, though not a moral judgment as Nast would have done. Over-large heads and exaggerated features make both men appear grotesque and their motions and postures border on the slapstick. Equally intriguing is the "comic-strip" format, a style few cartoonists before Stephans had adopted. Also ingenious is the script with its minimal text of puns; unlike the cartoons of many contemporaries, the artist's captions complement the pictorial humor of the satire. M.S.

A FIGHT FOR THE CHAMPIONSHIP

Thomas Nast. "The Political Death of the Bogus Caesar". (1869). Wood engraving. Plate dimensions, 9¼₆ × 13⅝". Collection The General Library, University of California, Berkeley. Appeared in *Harper's Weekly*, March 13, 1869.

*

With President Andrew Johnson's departure from office, Nast rejoiced. Snatching a Shakespearean allusion for his theme, his cartoon shows the tyrant Johnson lying dead among his vetoes, as assassins—including six of the seven managers of impeachment a year before—brandish their bloody daggers. Thaddeus Stevens, the leading radical Republican among them, strides away; by the time Johnson left office, his old enemy had died. On the wall, with obvious irony, the President's quote that "Treason is a Crime and must be punished" overview the "traitor" who received his due.

In this cartoon Nast imitated Gerome's famous painting, *Death of Caesar*, and he kept his own style similar to that of the original. Instead of the linear style with which he was familiar, Nast used half-tones achieved by drawing the scene on the woodblock with a brush; indeed, this method remained a favorite Nast technique through 1869, even as the complexity of his cartoons decreased.

Nast saw Johnson's political death as a great moral victory. Yet he held no grudges. Years later when Johnson returned to the capitol as a senator, the cartoonist drew himself bowing to his old enemy as Johnson proudly strode past, Constitution under his arm. It is said that on seeing it Johnson commented, "I forgive Nast everything he has done to me." Considering the effectiveness of Nast's work, that was quite a concession. M.S.

THE POLITICAL DEATH OF THE BOGUS CAESAR

"Liberty! Freedom! Tyranny is dead!
Run hence, proclaim, cry it about the streets."

THE POLITICAL DEATH OF THE BOGUS CÆSAR.

" Some to the common pulpits, and cry out
LIBERTY, FREEDOM, AND ENFRANCHISEMENT!"

164   HARPER'S WEEKLY.   [MARCH 13, 1869.

1869-1901

Ulysses S. Grant to William McKinley

Thomas Nast. "The 'Liberal' Conspirators (Who, You All Know, are Honorable Men)". Wood engraving. Plate dimensions, 10¹³⁄₁₆ × 15⁹⁄₁₆". Collection The General Library, University of California, Berkeley. Appeared in *Harper's Weekly*, March 16, 1872.

*

The "Liberal Conspirators" Nast depicts are all leading senators out of patience with President Grant. Eager to find an advocate to trumpet their charges, they consider editor Horace Greeley. Nast objected to the liberals because they opposed his idol, Grant. Although he shows none of the senators as "honorable men," many were men of high principle, aghast at the post-war corruption. They feared that the President had too much power and could get exactly what he wanted from Congress—like "Caesar with a Senate at his heel," as Charles Sumner put it.   M.S.

THE "LIBERAL" CONSPIRATORS (WHO, YOU ALL KNOW, ARE HONORABLE MEN)

THE "LIBERAL" CONSPIRATORS (WHO, YOU ALL KNOW, ARE HONORABLE MEN).

"'O, LET US HAVE HIM; FOR HIS SILVER HAIR   IT SHALL BE SAID, HIS JUDGMENT RUL'D OUR HANDS;
WILL PURCHASE US A GOOD OPINION,   OUR YOUTHS, AND WILDNESS, SHALL NO WHIT APPEAR,
AND BUY MEN'S VOICES TO COMMEND OUR DEEDS   BUT ALL BE BURIED IN HIS GRAVITY.'—*Julius Cæsar.*

HARPER'S WEEKLY.

[MARCH 16, 1872.

Matt Morgan. "Our Modern Belshazzar. The People's Handwriting on the Wall". (1872). Wood engraving. 13½ × 18". Collection The University of Chicago Library. Appeared in *Frank Leslie's Illustrated Weekly*, April 6, 1872.

*

As this cartoon demonstrates, Matt Morgan could outdo even Nast in savagery. Sprawled besotted on a throne protected by bayonets, President Ulysses S. Grant accepts "2nd Term" whiskey from his crony Senator Roscoe Conkling, and embraces the corrupt head of the New York customhouse. Other minor politicians support him: Morton leans on his crutch, Carpenter sits holding his belly and Chandler squats atop Senator Henry Wilson (both of them nearly in a stupor). The Vice-President, a devout Methodist, prays. Gifts and grafting surround the imperial despot, but in the main hall, angry liberal Republicans Sumner, Schurz, Trumbull and Fenton point to the handwriting on the wall, the declaration of party independence of Missouri's liberal Republican governor.

Employed at the English magazine *Fun* during the 1860s, Morgan emigrated to America in the early 1870s—just in time to serve as *Frank Leslie's Illustrated Weekly's* rival for Nast. Lacking the wit and sarcasm that gave Nast so much of his bite, Morgan's style altered in his new surroundings to take on many of Nast's characteristics: note the grandiose setting and the reliance on a multiplicity of figures. A mature draftsman, Morgan gave his sordid figures a compelling vividness.   M.S.

OUR MODERN BELSHAZZAR. THE PEOPLE'S HANDWRITING ON THE WALL

OUR MODERN BELSHAZZAR.

THE PEOPLE'S HANDWRITING ON THE WALL

James A. Wales. "The 'Strong' Government 1869-1877 — The 'Weak' Government 1877-1880". (1880). Color lithograph (silked). Plate dimensions, 14⁹⁄₁₆ × 18½". Collection The General Library, University of California, Berkeley. Appeared in *Puck*, May 12, 1880.

*

This cartoon contrasts the southern policies of Ulysses S. Grant with Rutherford B. Hayes. Hayes, an Ohio Republican, assumed the Presidency in 1876. The Republican and Democratic leaders had made a bargain that if the Democrats accepted Hayes as President, he would put an end to national interference in the South. This signified the end of "reconstruction," and the old-time Southern Democrats resumed control of their state governments. One result of this was that, in spite of the 15th Amendment which gave blacks the right to vote, state administration without federal intervention nullified the rights guaranteed by the Constitution.

Puck's editorial viewpoint supported Hayes' policy rather than Grant's. Grant's strong government was supported by carpetbaggers and bayonets, whereas Hayes' weak government was plowing under the bloody shirt, the symbol of sectional strife, and bringing forth a new era.   L.A./L.H.

THE "STRONG" GOVERNMENT 1869-1877 — THE "WEAK" GOVERNMENT 1877-1880

PUCK.

THE "STRONG" GOVERNMENT 1869–1877.

THE "WEAK" GOVERNMENT 1877–1881.

Joseph Keppler. "The Cinderella of the Republican Party and Her Haughty Sisters". (1880). Color lithograph (silked). Plate dimensions, 18⁹⁄₁₆ × 11⅜". Collection The General Library, University of California, Berkeley. Appeared in *Puck*, October 13, 1880.

*

Hayes assumed office after eight years of the corrupt Grant administration. The disputed election against Tilden clouded his title to office and weakened his position as President. Although a man of high standards of public and private morality, Hayes was a mediocre President who played a role subordinate to Congress throughout his term.

"The Cinderella of the Republican Party and Her Haughty Sisters" depicts the division within the Republican Party between the so-called "Stalwarts" and the "Half-Breeds." The Stalwart wing, represented by former President Grant and Roscoe Conkling, are trying to attract attention while Hayes, a Half-Breed, sits in the corner unnoticed. These factions had no political or economic convictions and were linked together solely for personal advantage or partisan purposes. While "Cinderella" Hayes takes care of his "prosperity soup" and keeps his house in order, his fellow Republicans, Grant and Conkling, ignore his efforts. Hayes' personal qualities like his "hard work marmalade" and the "good tempered preserves" can be seen on the top shelf in the kitchen.

Joseph Keppler took inspiration for many of his cartoons from the theater. The large colorful tableaux which he favored, like this one, were splendid showcases for Keppler's witty and appealing sense of theatrics. No other publication showed the same concern for colored illustrations as did *Puck*. Throughout the seventeen years that Keppler was art editor of *Puck*, his enthusiasm for brightly colored cartoons waxed and waned. By 1880 he was no longer content with simple tints. His use of a prevailing color, in this case, blue, to coordinate a scene owes as much of a debt to his years as a set designer in Vienna as does the stage-like composition itself.   L.A./L.H.

THE CINDERELLA OF THE REPUBLICAN PARTY AND HER HAUGHTY SISTERS

THE CINDERELLA OF THE REPUBLICAN PARTY AND HER HAUGHTY SISTERS.

Joseph Keppler. "On the Road". (1881). Color lithograph (silked). Plate dimensions, 11¼ × 18⅝". Collection The General Library, University of California, Berkeley. Appeared in *Puck*, February 2, 1881.

*

"On the Road" captures the factionalism within the Republican Party between the "Half-Breeds," represented by President Garfield, and the "Stalwarts," represented by Roscoe Conkling. Garfield, heading down the "rocky road to the White House," is met by Conkling, who wants to show him the way. Garfield asserts his strength against Conkling by refusing his offer.

Keppler was the first artist in America to apply color lithography to political cartoons, and he was forever tinkering with the magazine's color reproductions. For a time, he prepared not only the black and white lithograph stones, but the colored stones as well. "On the Road" is very likely one of these. Keppler liked to show off his artistic aspirations and would insert a landscape whenever the opportunity could be found. This gave his cartoons a spatial orientation rare in cartoons. His ambitions were the despair of *Puck's* business manager, Adolph Swartzmann, however, because Keppler's experiments and his finesse added enormously to production costs. Nonetheless, *Puck* was marketed at a price (10¢) which would attract the people who could not afford to buy the more expensive "art" magazines like *Harper's Weekly* (priced at a high 35¢). L.A./L.H.

ON THE ROAD.
CONKLING: "Want a Guide, Sir?" — GARFIELD: "No, thank you!"

Joseph Keppler. "A Presidential Conjurer".
(1881). Color lithograph (silked). Plate dimensions, 11⅜ × 18½". Collection The
General Library, University of California,
Berkeley. Appeared in *Puck*, October 12,
1881.

*

Trying to put an end to the patronage system, President Chester Arthur brought
about the first effective Civil Service Reform Act. As the cartoon suggests, it would
have taken a feat of magic to satisfy all the
factions within the Republican Party who
expected favors from him.

Keppler was partial to large compositions
with many figures. Unlike other satiric artists such as Daumier, Thomas Rowlandson
or George Luks, who used crowds as essays
on social morality, Keppler was never interested in drawing crowds for their own sake;
his crowd compositions are always dominated by an overriding political point.
L.A./L.H.

A PRESIDENTAL CONJUROR.
WHAT MR. ARTHUR MUST BE 'D SATISFY ALL THE POLITICIANS.

James A. Wales. "The Proper Thing". (1881). Color lithograph (silked). Plate dimensions, 19¹¹⁄₁₆ × 12⅜". Collection The General Library, University of California, Berkeley. Appeared in *Judge*, November 19, 1881.

*

"The Proper Thing" shows the transformation which occurred once Chester Arthur took office. Though Arthur had been known as a machine politician in New York, he dignified his image once he became President. His old chums—the New York spoilsmen—are asking Arthur for favors. They are trying to unlock his old image, but Arthur is no longer available. The sign posted on the outside of the door represents the change which has taken place now that he is President. He no longer wants to be "Chet Arthur" but rather "his Excellency—Chester A. Arthur." Arthur's desire to establish a dignified role for the President was partly a result of his own vanity, but it is also an example of what "the Presidency" can do to the men who hold this office. Its demands often produce unsuspected characteristics.

James A. Wales was one of the few American-born cartoonists who worked for the comic weeklies during the later decades of the century. He drew for *Puck* under Joseph Keppler's direction until 1881 when, confident that the country could support two comic weeklies based on the same format, he founded *Judge*. Wales, however, lacked Keppler's greater gifts and the publication was so financially unstable that in 1895 he sold it to a promoter who hired another *Puck* artist, Bernard Gillam, as art editor. Wales then returned to *Puck*.

Wales possessed a special gift for portraiture seen to advantage in this cartoon in Arthur's head, which peers above the door like an animated owl. He was also able to use verbal witticisms effectively and if his drawing lacks the accomplishment of other artists, his rather dry humor is nonetheless attractive.   L.A./L.H.

THE PROPER THING

THE PROPER THING.

Joseph Keppler. "King Chester Arthur's Knight(cap)s of the Round Table". (1882). Color lithograph (silked). Plate dimensions, 11³⁄₁₆ × 18⅝". Collection The General Library, University of California, Berkeley. Appeared in *Puck*, February 15, 1882.

*

The cartoon shows the responsibilities of leading the nation being neglected while Chester Arthur and his cabinet sleep. The foremost concern of the Arthur administration was to preserve peace and stay out of foreign entanglements; and America's foreign policy was simply expressed by the slogan, "No ill-will to anyone." Puck was disturbed, specifically, that the U.S. refused to do anything about the tyrannies of the Austrian Emperor and the Russian Czar, whose portraits were shown hanging on the wall.

The cartoon is an especially fine example of Keppler's positive understanding of chromolithography.   L.A./L.H.

KING CHESTER ARTHUR'S KNIGHT(CAP)S OF THE ROUND TABLE

KING CHESTER ARTHUR'S KNIGHT(CAP)S OF THE ROUND TABLE.

Joseph Keppler. "The National Grab Bag—
Help Yourself!" (1890). Color lithograph.
13¾ × 20". Collection Stanford University
Libraries, Stanford, California. Appeared
in *Puck*, April 16, 1890.

*

During Harrison's administration, the treasury surplus which had been built up during
Cleveland's first administration, disappeared. This cartoon shows little Harrison,
under the direction of his two colleagues,
the bulky Tom Reed and tall J. J. Ingalls,
senator from Kansas, allowing the surplus
funds to be grabbed by special interests.
The fifty-first or "Billion Dollar Congress"
spent the surplus lavishly. Appropriations
for river improvements, for coastal defenses,
and for federal buildings increased at such
speed that within two years the government
was in need of funds.

Keppler was most comfortable working
with personalities. In his better cartoons he
usually reconstructed political realities into
scenarios which took the form of a dialogue
between political principals in a social situation. He did not have a gift for abstract
analysis of issues, and "The National Grab
Bag" is a clever solution for his own limita-
tions. Rather than invent a symbolical or
schematic "bill," Keppler chose to represent
the legislative process by people. Each "bill"
is endowed with its own personal character
and like actors on a stage, they move across
the page. The legislative and executive
branches of government are neatly tele-
scoped into three personalities, Ingalls,
Harrison, and Reed. It is a cartoon executed with a clarity of thought and design
which is easily understood. L.A./L.H.

The National Grab Bag—Help Yourself!

Joseph Keppler. "The Raven". (1890). Color lithograph. 20 × 13¼". Collection Stanford University Libraries, Stanford, California. Appeared in *Puck*, August 13, 1890.

*

Benjamin Harrison, an Ohio Republican, represented conservative business interests. Like the other Presidents of the period, Harrison did not possess any special capabilities which would enable him to assume the leadership of the United States. His main attribute was that his grandfather, William Henry Harrison, had been President in 1841.

"The Raven" was inspired by the disagreement between President Harrison and James Blaine, Secretary of State, over their separate views on the McKinley Tariff. The McKinley Tariff was a bill to protect domestic manufacture from foreign competitors by raising the duties on imports. Harrison stood for high protection whereas Blaine believed in granting concessions which would permit reciprocity with other nations. Blaine is depicted as the "Raven" who is perched on the bust of former President William Henry Harrison.

Literary allusion in political cartoons was common in the nineteenth century. But in the famous "Raven," Keppler raised allusion into something approaching poetic vision. The deep shadows of the darkened room do not conjure up a sense of horror, but the details of the composition unmistakably imply the presence of the irrational for comic ends. Not funny, the cartoon is a witty idea which is communicated with a startling and unexpected technical accomplishment.
L.A./L.H.

PUCK.

THE RAVEN.

And the lamplight o'er him streaming   Throws his shadow on the floor;   And my soul from out that shadow   That lies floating on the floor
Shall be lifted — Nevermore!

Horace Taylor. "The Trust Giant's Point of View". (1900). Color offset-lithograph. 12¼ × 18½". Collection University of California, Los Angeles, Library. Appeared in *The Verdict*, January 22, 1900.

*

The corporation had become the dominant form of business organization by the 1900s. The Standard Oil Company had been the first to form a trust in 1879; and in that year Rockefeller controlled about 90% of America's refining industry. Although the Sherman Anti-Trust Law was passed in 1890, it was never enforced. Thus, the few wealthy industrialists who controlled corporations and monopolized the industry were able to reap high profits at the expense of the consumer. The laissez-faire economic policies of the day placed no controls on "big business."

This cartoon epitomizes the relationship between business and politics at the turn of the century. The President lies powerless in the hands of corporate power, represented by Rockefeller and his Standard Oil Empire. The Standard Oil Refinery has taken over the Capitol; it is directing the course of the government. Oil barrels surround the area and the sky is black with pollution.

A long, bitter editorial accompanied this cartoon which laid the blame for all the country's ills on McKinley and the Republican party (which the *Verdict* characteristically identified as "Hanna's party"). Horace Taylor was quite inventive and he had a knack for the double page cartoon, a skill he gained apparently from studying Joseph Keppler's designs for *Puck*. Using only minimal caricature, Taylor has managed with wit and style to insinuate by his design in just whose hands the government lay. Although by 1900 most of the important cartoonists were working in black and white at the daily newspapers, cartoons like this one indicate that the large colored cartoon was still a creative medium.   L.A./L.H.

THE TRUST GIANT'S POINT OF VIEW

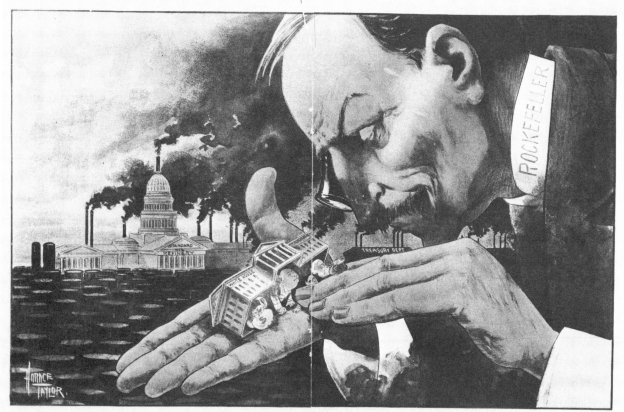

THE TRUST GIANT'S POINT OF VIEW.
"WHAT A FUNNY LITTLE GOVERNMENT!"

Horace Taylor. "The Battery of Imperialism". (1900). Color offset-lithograph. 12⅜ × 18⅝". Collection University of California, Los Angeles, Library. Appeared in *The Verdict*, March 26, 1900.

*

The United States joined the imperialistic powers in 1900, after the Spanish-American War. Besides spreading its influence in Cuba, Puerto Rico, Guam, the Phillipines and Hawaii, the U.S. also helped to suppress the Boxer Rebellion in China. The United States was on its way to becoming a world power.

The Verdict chose to believe that McKinley had imperialist ambitions and thus he frequently was made to appear as an emperor. He even more frequently appeared in the company of Marcus Hanna, a Cleveland capitalist, who was singled out for particular abuse by the magazine's cartoonists. Hanna, machine politics, and the party bosses are seen by *The Verdict* as the real villains of the political scene—not the President, who is usually the accomplice rather than the creator of villainy. Alfred Henry Lewis, editor of *The Verdict* and a passionate Democrat, believed that the solution for the country's problems lay in the old-fashioned Yankee virtue of self-determinism. Machine politics were, therefore, an insult to the principles of democratic government. L.A./L.H.

THE VERDICT.

THE BATTERY OF IMPERIALISM.

MAC TO MARK: "YOU'VE FIXED THEM SO THEY LOOK ALL RIGHT; BUT I WONDER WHICH WAY THE BLAMED THINGS ARE GOING TO SHOOT!"

Joseph Keppler. "Where is He?" (1892). Color lithograph (silked). 19¾ × 13⅜". Collection The General Library, University of California, Berkeley. Appeared in *Puck*, November 16, 1892.

*

In "Where is He?" Harrison is so insignificant that the government runs without him and his absence is not even felt. During this period, the "Presidency was not viewed as operating at the center of national affairs; government in the dominant attitudes of the day was a peripheral activity. Politics did not attract men of imagination and creative leadership because government was not seen as a place where such qualities were needed."[1] Power rested with Congress —and especially the Senate—rather than with the President.

Early in the 1880s, *Puck* initiated trademarks for certain prominent political figures. For Harrison, the magazine hit upon his grandfather's (President William H. Harrison's) hat, which began appearing immediately after his election in 1888. By the end of his term in 1892, *Puck* had cheerfully traced Harrison's desultory performance by progressively shrinking his diminutive figure and enlarging the hat. When Cleveland was elected in November 1892, the motif came to its logical conclusion, and Harrison disappeared altogether. It took a bit of experimenting for Keppler to arrive at the perfect conclusion to the contrivance, however; in an early version worked in watercolor, Harrison still appears dangling below the hat. The final version is one of his most famous and appealing designs, and is remarkable for its simplicity and wit.   L.A./L.H.

1. James MacGregor Burns, *Presidential Government* (Boston, 1973), p. 55.

PUCK.

"WHERE IS HE?"

Bernard Gillam. "The New Capitol". (1894). Lithograph. 13¼ × 20½". Collection Riverside City & County Public Library. Appeared in *Judge*, August 11, 1894.

*

Cleveland returned to office for a second term in 1893, following Benjamin Harrison's Presidency. Cleveland's second administration was plagued with two major economic problems: the tariff and the currency. Cleveland favored a reduction in the tariff unlike the Republicans who supported a high tariff in order to protect U.S. industry from foreign competition. The currency problem concerned the battle between gold and silver. Cleveland defended the gold standard despite the effects it was having on the farmers.

The central issue of this cartoon concerns the "tariff problem." While Cleveland is shown asserting his executive power in all the branches of the government, in reality, he believed in the theory of the separation of powers. In front of the "Cleveland Capitol" stand Senators White, Vest, McPherson, Daniel, Brice, Gordon and Harris. They are headed by Senator Gorman of Maryland, the leader of the Democratic Protectionists in the Senate. These senators favored a high tariff which would benefit the industrialists. The Wilson-Gorman Act of 1894 replaced the McKinley Tariff although it did not make any serious change in the nature of tariff legislation. These senators were supported by some of the most powerful economic interests in the country. Senator Murphy, pictured on the right, represented the collar and cuff manufacturers.

Judge enjoyed mistaking Cleveland's physical corpulence for political grossness. But in spite of *Judge's* anti-Democratic bias, the tone of the cartoons remained jocular rather than condemning. Like most of the other comic weeklies, *Judge* was seldom a forum for a particular political program, and caricature was employed primarily for its comic aspect. Gillam's cartoons complemented this editorial tendency to mollify political criticism; his treatment of Cleveland and his supporters is censorious, but droll.
L.A./L.H.

THE NEW CAPITOL

THE NEW CAPITOL.

CASSIUS (*Gorman*)—"He doth bestride the narrow world like a Colossus; and we petty men walk under his huge legs, and peep
about to find ourselves dishonorable graves. Upon what meat doth this our Cæsar feed that he is grown so great?"—*Shakespeare*.

George Luks. "Hanna: That Man Clay Was an Ass. It's Better to be President than to be Right!" (1899). Color offset-lithograph. 12⅞₁₆ × 9½". Collection University of California, Los Angeles, Library. Appeared in *The Verdict*, March 18, 1899.

*

It was no secret that Senator Henry Clay wanted, above all else, to be President. Yet he was never nominated. Clay believed that the reason for this was due to his outspoken stance on various unpopular issues; and his consolation was expressed in his famous declaration, "It's better to be right, than to be President."

Cartoonist George Luks used this famous statement to express his feelings about President McKinley and Senator Marcus Hanna, a wealthy Ohio industrialist. Both men exemplified the union between politics and big business; they each felt that the government existed to protect, encourage and fortify business. The caption for the cartoon, "Hanna: That Man Clay Was an Ass/It's Better to be President than to be Right!", expresses the two men's attitude toward Clay's unselfish attitude. By implication, McKinley and Hanna are seen as self-serving individuals, sacrificing what is "right" for their own selfish ends.

"That Man Clay Was an Ass" is one of the strongest cartoons which George Luks drew for *The Verdict*. The strength of the characterizations—Hanna as a gross, greuling monster, McKinley as a shabby ineffectual President—is typical of *The Verdict*. Essentially, the magazine was founded to work for McKinley's defeat in 1900 and most of the cartoons were drawn for that end. Although it followed the format of other New York comic weeklies, *The Verdict* insisted on being taken seriously. It called itself "a political, but *not* a *comic*, paper" and "a paper to make you think." Think Democrat, that is. The fierce partisan interest of the magazine encouraged savagery from its cartoonists; some are among the most powerful images published in American journalism before the appearance of the *Masses*. L.A./L.H.

HANNA: THAT MAN CLAY WAS AN ASS. IT'S BETTER TO BE PRESIDENT THAN TO BE RIGHT!

HANNA: THAT MAN CLAY WAS AN ASS. IT'S BETTER TO BE PRESIDENT THAN TO BE RIGHT!

Horace Taylor. "Republicanism Down to Date". (1899). Color offset-lithograph. 12½ × 18⅜". Collection University of California, Los Angeles, Library. Appeared in *The Verdict*, September 25, 1899.

*

From the close of the Civil War until 1890, the United States was primarily concerned with its own internal development. Yet once its continental frontiers had been reached and industrialization had been established, the United States became interested in overseas expansion.

As a result of the Spanish-American War, the United States had established a colonial empire with firm control of the Caribbean and possessions in the western Pacific. McKinley had at first been opposed to war with Spain and to annexation of overseas territories, but he soon bent to the pressures from various Republican senators, cabinet members John Hay and Elihu Root, religious evangelists and the press. His will was similarly maleable regarding the interests of big business. This cartoon reflects the dominance of imperialism and the trusts under McKinley and the earlier Republican administrations.

Like many of *The Verdict's* cartoons, this particular one has the strength of statement and uses the kinds of symbols typical of the radical press. However, the editorial policy of *The Verdict* was not in the least radical. The publication worked for nothing more revolutionary than the defeat of McKinley in the coming election. Thus *The Verdict* had no real program of social or political reform. Confined to a narrow partisan interest, floated by a wealthy financier, lacking the commitment and energy of the radical press,

and somewhat embarrassed about being funny like the mass magazines, *Puck*, *Judge*, and *Life*, *The Verdict* apparently never solicited and never gained wide circulation. Taylor's considerable gifts for design and his ability to reduce political subjects to pathos might have served to bring him out of the obscurity of this little known magazine had the comic weeklies been less lighthearted, or had the journals of the left employed cartoonists. As it was, he seems to have dropped from sight when *The Verdict* folded.   L.A./L.H.

THE VERDICT.

REPUBLICANISM DOWN TO DATE.
HANNA: "DON'T BE AFRAID, MACK; IT WON'T MAKE MUCH NOISE!"

Horace Taylor. "After the Feast. The Working Man Gets What is Left!" (1899). Color offset-lithograph. 12¼ × 18½". Collection University of California, Los Angeles, Library. Appeared in *The Verdict*, December 4, 1899.

*

With industrialization came growing discrepancies in the social classes. As leaders of industry grew richer, the workers were unable to share a great part of the wealth. This cartoon shows the social inequality between the rich industrialists and the starving laborer. McKinley worked closely with the nation's business interests and neglected the concerns of the workers. Business was responsible for low wages, irregular employment, unprotected machinery, unsanitary factories and crowded sweatshops which undermined the living conditions of industrial workers.

Like *Puck* and *Judge*, *The Verdict* published three colored cartoons weekly which were printed on the cover and inside centerfold. The technology of color reproduction had become more sophisticated by the end of the century, and *The Verdict's* cartoons show an interesting advancement in their use of half-tones.

Cartoonist Horace Taylor also had a happy understanding of the design potential of the double page spread, and his work as a cartoonist is distinguished by a remarkable ability to utilize the magazine's center spread for polemic ends. The composition here is legible and condemning; a starving laborer is pitted against a glut of fat cats and their steward, the implacable McKinley. The caricature is malevolent and the caption bitter and ironic. It is a very persuasive piece of visual propaganda; and yet, the conception has wit enough to relieve the cartoon from factional dreariness.   L.A./L.H.

AFTER THE FEAST. THE WORKING MAN GETS WHAT IS LEFT!

THE VERDICT.

AFTER THE FEAST.
THE WORKING MAN GETS WHAT IS LEFT!

1901-1933
Theodore Roosevelt to Herbert Hoover

Gustav Brandt. "Theodore Roosevelt, President of the United States". (n.d.). Photographic reproduction of the published version of the cartoon which appeared in *Kladeradatsch* [Berlin].

*

Gustav Brandt of *Kladeradatsch* (a German humor magazine on the model of *Punch* and *Charivari)* portrayed Roosevelt in a powerful caricature. This carefully drawn image is basically naturalistic, except for two major distortions: the mouth and the pose of the body which captures the essential impression of Roosevelt's manner as a public speaker. Photographs of Roosevelt speaking verify that he often actually did lean far over the podium, gesturing and working his face wildly.

The contortion of pose and expression in this drawing suggest ties with German Expressionism, a growing movement at this time; although the more restrained style of drawing is unlike the harsh, rough brush strokes or woodcut lines typical of Expressionist art. German political cartoons of the early twentieth century seem to have been more closely linked to contemporary artistic trends than were most American cartoons. A.H.

THEODORE ROOSEVELT, PRESIDENT OF THE UNITED STATES

THEODORE ROOSEVELT, PRESIDENT OF THE UNITED STATES

L. C. Gregg. "For President!" (c. 1904). Photographic reproduction of the published version of the cartoon which appeared in the *Atlanta Constitution.*

*

One of Roosevelt's goals in public life was to instill in the national character "heroic virtues" and to bring back what he called "the fighting edge." His own activities as a cowboy, frontiersman, hunter, naval hero and cavalryman, made Roosevelt the object of much admiration and idolization. Yet at the same time, others saw Roosevelt's love of excitement, fighting, and power as an affinity for violence. In 1897, when he was Secretary of the Navy, Roosevelt made a classic militaristic speech before the Naval War College in which he dwelt on the superiority of military to pecuniary values.[1] He delcared it was more dangerous that a nation be over-pacific than over-warlike. To cartoonist L. C. Gregg, Roosevelt as President meant the institutionalization of militarism, imperialism, chauvinism and ultra-nationalism.   G.K.

1. Richard Hofstadter, *The American Political Tradition* (Revised edition, New York, 1973), p. 213.

L. C. Gregg in the Atlanta *Constitution*.

FOR PRESIDENT!

Thomas Theodor Heine. "Präsident Roosevelts Alpdrücken" ["President Roosevelt's Nightmare"]. (1907). Linoleum block print. Plate dimensions, 9⁵⁄₁₆ × 7¹⁵⁄₁₆". Collection The General Library, University of California, Berkeley. Appeared in *Simplicissimus*, March 11, 1907.

*

Following his 1904 reelection, Roosevelt plunged into international activity when the Japanese secretly asked him to initiate treaty negotiations of the Russo-Japanese War. The Japanese were the victors in the war, yet they found they had to settle for far less than they had originally hoped. They put much of the blame on Roosevelt's role in the talks, causing an outbreak of anti-American sentiment in Japan. In turn, American prejudice against the Japanese, already widespread on the West Coast, increased as people came to fear what they termed the "yellow peril." Much racist activity followed, the most blatant occurring in October, 1906, when the San Francisco Board of Education ordered that the ninety-three Japanese children in their schools be segregated into a separate school. The hostile feelings already astir in Japan swelled, with the tensions culminating in speculations of war between the two powers.

Thomas Theodor Heine depicts this nightmare of an incident to be President Roosevelt's. Although he claimed to be disturbed by the school board's action, Roosevelt found he was essentially powerless in dealing with the state's public schools. As the situation worsened, Roosevelt continued to apply pressure, and finally succeeded in maneuvering the California officials into revoking the damaging action. He promised them that the influx of Japanese immigrants —the "yellow peril"—would end. Japan's share of the cost came in 1907, when Roosevelt devised a "gentleman's agreement" whereby Japan was required to halt the issuance of passports to Japanese workers wishing to emigrate to the United States.

The idea of representing the Japanese as slant-eyed yellow cats provided a perfect outlet for Thomas Theodor Heine for two reasons: he was an expert at drawing animals, and he liked to incorporate vivid colors into his cartoons. The result was this striking composition of sinuous interlocking shapes of black, lavender, and bright yellow. The decorative pattern created by the cats seems to have been one of Heine's foremost aims in drawing this cartoon.

This decorative quality is typical of the "Simplicissimus style" of cartooning, a movement of great importance to twentieth-century caricature in Germany and all over the world. The political-satirical weekly *Simplicissimus* had been founded in 1896, the same year in which *Jugend*, a similar magazine also published in Munich, first appeared. The art work published in these magazines was so distinctive that the Art Noveau movement in Germany was referred to as *Jugendstil*. The realm of caricature was particularly identified with *Simplicissimus* because of the outstanding cartoonists it employed.   A.H./G.K.

Präsident Roosevelts Alpdrücken

(Zeichnung von Th. Th. Heine)

Die Japaner kommen!

William A. Rogers. "The First Spadeful". (n.d.). Ink on paper. 17⅛ × 21". Collection Library of Congress. Reproduced in the *New York Herald*, date unknown.

*

The way in which Theodore Roosevelt acquired the Panama Canal Zone for the United States, advantageous as it was, has been considered one of the most shameful and discreditable episodes in American history. After deciding that the route through Panama would be the best for the needed canal route, Roosevelt agreed to pay off the French company which had the original rights to the canal, but made no arrangements with the Colombian government which owned the land. When the Colombian government hesitated to sign over the land to the U.S., Roosevelt became outraged, referring to the Colombians as "those contemptible little creatures in Bogota." Then, when a Panamanian revolution for independence from Colombia conveniently broke out, Roosevelt sent U.S. warships to the Isthmus to aid in the overthrow of Colombian sovereignty. The Panamanians formed the Republic of Panama which, for a guarantee of its independence, gave the United States complete authority over the canal. Thus, in 1904 the dirt began to fly in Panama. Despite the ill will it brought the United States, Roosevelt remained convinced he was right and later boasted, "I took the Isthmus, started the Canal, and then left Congress—not to debate the Canal —but to debate me."

This cartoon shows, through an emphasis on Roosevelt's size, the importance he and the U.S. Navy played in the affair. Since the new Panamanian government signed the treaty with the United States while communication lines to the Colombian capital of Bogota were still cut off, the delay in communication is also suggested.   G.K.

THE FIRST SPADEFUL

Artist Unknown. "A Nauseating Job, but it Must Be Done". (n.d.). Photographic reproduction of the published version of the cartoon which appeared in the *Saturday Globe*.

*

At the turn of the century a reform movement began to sweep the country with journalists leading the investigations by publicizing the facts of the miserable, filthy, poverty-stricken side of American society. It was Theodore Roosevelt in a 1906 speech who first labelled those journalists "muckrakers." Roosevelt admitted that the muckrakers' attacks were valid, but he reacted negatively, fearing that the more moderate "Square Deal" he was offering the country might be jeopardized by their demands.

After he was elected as President in 1904, Roosevelt did undertake a more comprehensive program of reform than he had during the previous term with his Square Deal. He accomplished much in the areas of natural resource conservation, railroad regulation and what was the beginning of consumer protection. In June of 1905, for example, the first federal meat inspection law was passed. The muckrakers' protests were not curbed by this major piece of legislation, however, because the law called for the meat to be inspected at the government's expense. They felt that Roosevelt had buckled under and settled for far less than the "drastic and thoroughgoing" legislation that he had demanded.

Much of the credit for the progressive measures enacted during Roosevelt's administration was received by the President, rather than by the muckrakers themselves. Typically, this particularly pungent cartoon pictures Roosevelt personally taking charge of the Chicago packing-house muckraking investigation. B.W.

A Nauseating Job, but it Must Be Done

A NAUSEATING JOB, BUT IT MUST BE DONE

(President Roosevelt takes hold of the investigating muck-rake himself in the packing-house scandal.)

Joseph Keppler, Jr. "Martin Luther Roosevelt". Color lithograph; artist's proof. 12 × 18". Collection Mr. and Mrs. Draper Hill, Memphis, Tennessee. Reproduced in *Puck*, April 17, 1907.

*

In "Martin Luther Roosevelt" Keppler made use of a famous—though unsubstantiated—story regarding Martin Luther, the leader of the Protestant Revolt against the Catholic Church. Some people interpreted Luther's protests as the work of the Devil. As the story goes, when the Devil came into Luther's cell in the monastery to tempt him, his presence was so real that Luther threw his ink bottle at the apparition to chase it away. The ink splashed on the wall, where it can still be seen.

Having served the balance of assassinated President McKinley's term, and a full one of his own, Teddy Roosevelt declared that he would not be a candidate for another term. Yet in this cartoon, the Devil has appeared to tempt Roosevelt with a "Third Term." Tempting as a third term might be, however, Roosevelt stands firm in his convictions and, like Martin Luther, attempts to drive the Devil away by hurling his ink pot at him.

Four years later, however, the "temptation" proved too great. Dissatisfied with his successor's (Taft's) performance in office, Roosevelt again ran for President. Yet when his candidacy divided the vote, Woodrow Wilson became President.   T.B.

MARTIN LUTHER ROOSEVELT

PUCK

MARTIN LUTHER ROOSEVELT.

Oliver Herford. "William Howard Taft".
(1917). Photo-engraving after the original
drawing. Plate dimensions, 4⅞ × 4⅛". Collection The General Library, University of
California, Berkeley. Appeared in Herford's
book, *Confessions of a Caricaturist*, published in 1917.

*

This charming little caricature of Taft and
its accompanying quatrain exemplify the
way in which witty lines—both pictorial
and verbal—flowed from the pen of Oliver
Herford.

Taft actually was even more overweight
than this drawing suggests; at one time he
weighed 362 pounds. He was a genial President with an infectious laugh and an easy-
going personality, and had been a very
capable judge and administrator. But like
many of his predecessors, he was not very
well suited to the Presidency. He did not
have the ambition, the political skills, or
even the energy that should be demanded of
a successful President. Taft's administration
was undistinguished and troubled by his
lack of control over members of his own
party. Following upon the strong leadership
of Roosevelt he appeared especially weak.
A.H.

WILLIAM HOWARD TAFT

WILLIAM HOWARD TAFT
I'm sorry William Taft is out
Of Politics; without a doubt
Of all the Presidential crew
He was the easiest to do.

Joseph Keppler, Jr. "The Courtship of Bill Taft". (1907). Color offset-lithograph. 13¾ × 20½". Collection Stanford University Libraries, Stanford, California. Appeared in *Puck*, April 24, 1907.

*

As Theodore Roosevelt's first complete term as President neared an end, the Republican Party longed for the chance to renominate him. But on election day, 1904, Roosevelt had vowed that "under no circumstances" would he be a candidate for renomination. While he felt obliged to stand by this promise, he became convinced that he had to select his own successor.

Roosevelt's first preference was probably Secretary of State Elihu Root. But when Root chose not to run, Roosevelt's logical choice became William Howard Taft. Taft and Roosevelt were old friends, and Taft was an able administrator and an eminent jurist. Once he was selected by Roosevelt, there was never any question that Taft would win the Republican nomination. When the Republican convention met, the delegates merely confirmed Roosevelt's choice.

Joseph Keppler, Jr. conceived this cartoon from the near-perfect parallel of the fictitious theme of Longfellow's poem, "The Courtship of Miles Standish." Miles Standish, captain of the Plymouth colony, asks his better-educated friend, John Alden, to woo the maid, Priscilla Mullins, for him. Alden, who is also in love with Priscilla,

submits to his friend's wish and announces Standish's message. Priscilla then answers with her famous question, "Why don't you speak for yourself, John?" In the cartoon, "John Alden" Roosevelt asks the Republican Party (Priscilla) to nominate his best friend, "Miles Standish" Taft (in the background), as the 1908 candidate for President. The Republican Party, of course, would rather Roosevelt were asking for himself.
G.K.

THE COURTSHIP OF BILL TAFT

THE COURTSHIP OF BILL TAFT.

PRISCILLA. — Why don't you speak for yourself, Theodore?

Joseph Keppler, Jr. "Goodness Gracious! I Must Have Been Dozing!" (1910). Color offset-lithograph. 13¾ × 20½". Collection Stanford University Libraries, Stanford, California. Appeared in *Puck*, June 22, 1910.

*

When Theodore Roosevelt left office in 1908, he confidently promised that what he designated as "my policies" would be defended by his successor, William Howard Taft. But Roosevelt's last two years in office had been marked by a shift toward the left; and Taft—who was by nature a conservative—refused to continue the liberalizing trend. This created many conflicts and instabilities in the Republican Party, already in upheaval with a growing insurgency movement.

Taft had come to the Presidency with the pledge to achieve the Roosevelt policies as enunciated in 1906 and 1907. He had conscientiously worked to obtain them, and by 1910 had been successful to a surprising degree. But the reform movement made increasingly more radical demands and Taft responded in a reactionary manner. With Roosevelt's impelling personal influence removed (he was touring Africa and Europe), Taft had continued to drift steadily toward the right. By the summer of 1910, when this cartoon appeared, Taft was considered among the stand-pat Republicans and an opponent to the party's insurgents. And, as Taft's policies became less like "my policies" and represented more anti-Roosevelt positions, there formed a deep break between the former best friends.

Keppler's drawing of Taft as a dozing old woman shows him tangled in a web of yarn representing the issues that plagued his administration. Roosevelt looks in astonishment at the mess which Taft has made of his "My Policies" ball of yarn. Even Taft seems surprised that his lack of action—or dozing—has been the cause of the confusion. G.K.

GOODNESS GRACIOUS! I MUST HAVE BEEN DOZING!

PUCK

"GOODNESS GRACIOUS! I MUST HAVE BEEN DOZING!"

E. Hine. [Untitled caricature of Wilson and Taft]. (1912). Photo-engraving after the original drawing. 15⅜ × 10³⁄₁₆". Collection The General Library, University of California, Berkeley. Appeared in *Harper's Weekly*, August 10, 1912.

*

E. Hine. [Untitled caricature of Theodore Roosevelt]. (1912). Photo-engraving after the original drawing. 15⅜ × 10³⁄₁₆". Collection The General Library, University of California, Berkeley. Appeared in *Harper's Weekly*, August 17, 1912.

*

The 1912 Presidential campaign pitted former President Theodore Roosevelt, incumbent President William Howard Taft and Woodrow Wilson in a bitter fight. E. Hine drew these caricatures of the three candidates for a regular column in *Harper's Weekly* entitled "The Progress of the Campaign."

Hine was not a caricaturist who had a well-defined manner. But all of his drawings emphasize the use of suggestive lines, interspersed at times with flat areas, yet without any use of light and shade. This manner of drawing places Hine in the Art Nouveau tradition, with distinct traces of Aubrey Beardsley's style apparent as in the curvilinear, sinuous lines of the Taft caricature and the combination of linear and solid black in the Wilson drawing. Hine conveys the popular images of Roosevelt as the aggressive cowboy and Wilson as the puritanical professor. Taft, in turn, is a jolly but superficial Santa Claus type.   A.H.

Olaf Gulbransson. "Jezt ist Amerika schön in der Tinte!" ["Now America is Nicely in the Soup"]. (1914). Process engraving. Plate dimensions, 11⅝ × 7⅞". Collection The General Library, University of California, Berkeley. Appeared in *Simplicissimus*, May 11, 1914.

*

In 1913, Victoriano Huerta declared himself military dictator of Mexico. Wilson felt strongly that Huerta's regime should not be recognized by the United States, and in April 1914, he went so far as to forcefully intervene. When a shipload of ammunition was about to arrive at Veracruz, Wilson ordered the Navy to prevent the arms from reaching Huerta. In the ensuing action, carried out without Congressional approval, 19 Americans and 200 Mexicans were killed. Neither the Constitutionalists whom Wilson was trying to help, nor the rest of the world, approved Wilson's actions.

In the cartoon, "Professor Wilson"—who has been lecturing to the world about the immorality of military intervention—has spilled a bottle of blood-red ink on a map of Mexico. Literally translated, it says America is "in the ink"—a German idiom for being in trouble.

This cartoon is a fine example of the style of Olaf Gulbransson, a Norwegian caricaturist who joined the Munich magazine, *Simplicissimus* in 1902 and helped bring that magazine its fame. His style, closely tied to Art Nouveau or *Jugendstil*, is characterized by broad, flat areas of strong color and definite convoluted contours, which had a strong impact on the graphic art of the time. In this cartoon, the vivid, rather harsh colors and the wriggling lines create a strong psychological impact. Gulbransson once said that he worked more with an eraser than with a pencil; and the end product is this kind of drawing in which there is not one uncertain or extraneous line. Every detail contributes to the expressive quality of the whole.   A.H./B.W.

JEZT IST AMERIKA SCHÖN IN DER TINTE!

Professor Wilson

Zeichnung von O. Gulbransson

„Jetzt ist Amerika schön in der Tinte!"

Edward Thöny. "Die Enkel Washingtons" ["Washington's Grandson"]. (1915). Photo gravure. Plate dimensions, 11½ × 5⅝". Collection The General Library, University of California, Berkeley. Appeared in *Simplicissimus*, February 9, 1915.

*

This cartoon by Edward Thöny in *Simplicissimus* continues in the Art Nouveau or *Jugendstil* vein in German cartooning (see nos. 54 and 63). The curving line describing Wilson's upper sleeve is particularly calligraphic and reminiscent of the "whiplash" line so characteristic of Art Nouveau. Yet the face and hand are drawn in a very different, more realistic style. The face is modeled by areas of light and shade which are simplified into rather geometric forms, but which taken together create almost a naturalistic portrait, with only slight exaggeration of the features.

This cartoon depicts the pervasive feeling in Germany that Wilson's neutrality actually favored England. Here "Washington's Grandson" shows his dependence on Britain and his readiness to enter into open belligerency against Germany.   A.H./B.W.

Die Enkel Washingtons

(Zeichnung von E. Thöny)

„Meine Herren! Neutralitätsbruch zu Gunsten und mit Genehmigung Englands ist der einzige Akt von Freiheit, der uns auszuüben erlaubt ist. Wir können diesen letzten Rest von Macht nicht auch noch aufgeben!"

Jay N. Darling ["Ding"]. "When the Teacher Calls to Talk Things Over with Your Folks". (1919). Pen and ink on paper. 28½ × 22½". Collection The University of Iowa Libraries, Iowa City. Reproduced in the *Des Moines Register*, September 11, 1919.

*

Out of the destruction of the First World War came a movement to form a League of Nations. Wilson, the chief molder of the Treaty of Versailles, made the creation of a League an integral part of the Treaty. Although polls and newspaper estimates indicated that a majority of Americans originally supported the League, a stong bloc of Republican senators prevented the ratification of the Treaty, and support waned. In order to revive public enthusiasm for the League and bring pressure on the Senate, President Wilson embarked on an extended speaking tour of the United States in September of 1919. But the trip was cut short by Wilson's collapse which was followed by his partial paralysis and his subsequent incapacity to administer his office effectively.

In both content and drawing style, the cartoon is quite characteristic of Jay Darling. This work, by a typically American cartoonist, can be readily contrasted with the formal innovations achieved by European artists such as Edward Thöny (no. 64) and Olaf Gulbransson (no. 63).   A.H./B.W.

WHEN THE TEACHER CALLS TO TALK THINGS OVER WITH YOUR FOLKS

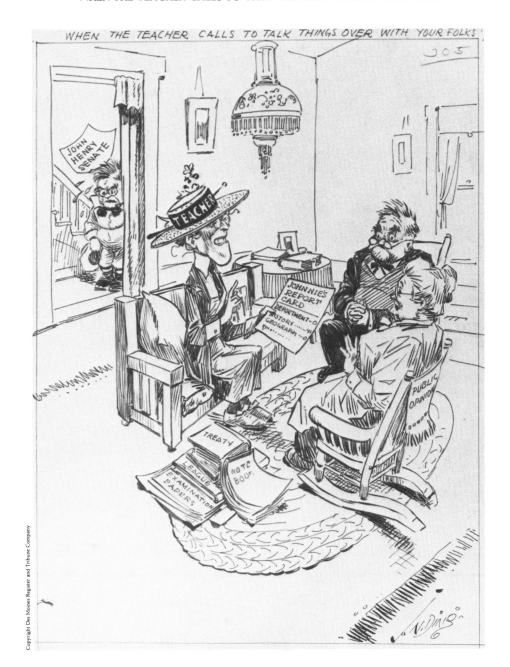

J. P. Alley. "The Candidate for Reelection".
(1923). Photographic reproduction of the
published version of the cartoon which appeared in *The Commercial Appeal*, February 8, 1923.

*

H. L. Mencken once wrote of Warren
Gamaliel Harding that, "Gamaliel is the
normal American of the better class—the
more honest and reflective class. His
thoughts are muddled, but profound. He
speaks bad English, but he has heart. He is
the archetype of the Homo boobus." The
election of Harding in 1920 ushered in a
new political era. The mandate of the voters
in that year was for a return to a simpler,
more private style of life, away from the
great campaigns of progressivism and "making the world safe for democracy." People
wanted to be left alone and not disturbed
by new crusades.

Harding's campaign slogan was "Back to
normalcy." Normalcy was not even a word
until Harding misread the word "normality"
in a speech someone wrote for him. When
this cartoon appeared, there was growing
controversy over whether Harding should
run for a second term. This Alley cartoon
is a comment on the accomplishments of
the Harding administration; the cartoonist
seems to have felt that most incumbents
run on their record while Harding could
only run on a slogan.   B.W.

THE CANDIDATE FOR REELECTION.

"I'll have to figure out some kind of a new slogan."

—Alley in the Memphis *Commercial-Appeal*.

Daniel Fitzpatrick. "The Cash Register Chorus". 1924. Ink, charcoal and opaque wash on paper. 20 × 17¾". Collection The State Historical Society of Missouri. Reproduced in the *St. Louis Post-Dispatch*, September 21, 1924.

*

The spirit of Calvin Coolidge's administration was best expressed in his famous statement that "the business of America is business." Coolidge felt that the prosperity of the nation could best be maintained by giving business all possible governmental support. The progressive tax policies of the Wilson administration were reversed, tariffs were raised, credit became more available to corporations, and anti-trust actions were non-existent. All of these policies contributed to the dramatic business boom of the Coolidge era. Although it was not recognized at that time, such policies also added to the basic economic unsoundness of the period, which culminated—after Coolidge had left office—in the crash of 1929 and the depression which followed.

Fitzpatrick's cartoon portrays a kind of barbershop quartet, the "Cash Register Chorus," gathered around a piano-sized cash register and singing the praises of Coolidge (alluding, of course, to the revival hymn "What a Friend We Have in Jesus"). These four corpulent, well-dressed men need no labels like "Trust" or "Big Business" as were often seen in earlier cartoons. By 1924 the public must have easily recognized this overfed type, and the cash register with the single dollar sign provides all the additional suggestion of moneyed interests that is needed. The President, Coolidge, does not appear in this cartoon except by name, which is typical of Fitzpatrick's cartooning: it nearly always deals with general issues and types of people rather than portraying a particular individual's actions.

Daniel Fitzpatrick's accomplished use of the crayon technique places him in the tradition of Daumier and other great lithographers. He expressed his idea in a quick series of broad, textured, sweeps of the crayon without extraneous detail. Fitzpatrick's talents were given recognition in 1926, when he received the Pulitzer Prize for Political Cartoons.   A.H.

Fitzpatrick in the St. Louis Post-Dispatch

THE CASH REGISTER CHORUS.

Robert Carter. "Tremble, Boys. Here's the Author of All Those Notes!" (1926). Newsprint clipping. 9½ × 8¼". Collection Library of Congress.

*

In spite of President Wilson's intervention in Mexico, until the American entry into World War I, most foreign observers felt him to be an impractical idealist, a weak and spineless leader who had no conception of the need to use force. Wilson consistently took no concrete actions against the repeated violations of America's neutral rights by both England and Germany. The President even declared, shortly after the sinking of the *Lusitania*, that "There is such a thing as a man being too proud to fight. There is such a thing as a nation being so right that it does not need to convince others by force that is right."

Robert Carter captures these ideas by comparing Wilson to Don Quixote — the idealistic dreamer who is really quite harmless in his persistent attacks on evil. Wilson, who often made broad moralizing speeches, is portrayed as the "Champion of Everything". The donkey he rides takes liberties with the Don Quixote allusion (the donkey was Sancho Panza's mount), but increases the ridicule of Wilson. The parody of Wilson as Cervantes' Don Quixote is a standard English stylistic device of the time; English cartoonists often utilized characters out of "classics" to mock their subjects. The characters used to symbolize Russia, Bulgaria, France, Germany, Mexico, England and Turkey were standard symbols for those nations at that time — just as "Uncle Sam" stood for the United States.   A.H./B.W.

TREMBLE, BOYS. HERE'S THE AUTHOR OF ALL THOSE NOTES!

"Tremble, Boys. Here's the Author of All Those Notes!"

Gluyas Williams. "Crisis in Washington".
(1929). Photo-engraving after the original
drawing. Plate dimensions, 8¾ × 7⅛".
Collection The General Library, University
of California, Berkeley. Appeared in *Life*,
February 15, 1929.

*

"Silent Cal" was definitely not a charismatic President. He had happened into the
office through his predecessor Harding's
death, and was reelected in 1924 because
the country was pleased with what was
called the "Coolidge prosperity" and because the Democratic Party was bitterly
split over Prohibition and the Ku Klux Klan.

Coolidge was reserved and formal with everyone but close friends. His puritanical
Vermont background was reflected in his
conscientious and frugal leadership. The
cartoon suggests an extension of the
Coolidge primness and frugality to a ludi-
crous degree

Gluyas Williams' drawing style is unique,
although its elimination of half-tones, its
careful pen lines, and its punctuation by
areas of solid black have a degree of similarity to some of his contemporaries (com-
pare for example, with nos. 54, 61A and B,
and 62). There is also a similarity to the
turn-of-the-century style of Aubrey Beardsley, whom Williams greatly admired. Every
line or spot of black is precisely placed to
contribute to a balanced and humorous
effect, and Williams fills the cartoon with
witty details. In the midst of all the bustling
activity sits Coolidge—prim, upright, and
frowning at the inefficiency of others which
delays him for a precisely arranged schedule.   A.H.

CRISIS IN WASHINGTON

Crisis In Washington

Mr. Coolidge refuses point blank to vacate the White House until his other rubber is found.

Paolo Garretto. "The President of the
United States, Herbert Clark Hoover, Looking Ahead Over the Top of a High Protective Collar". (1930). Newsprint clipping.
7¼ × 6½". Collection Herbert Hoover
Presidential Library. Appeared in the
New York World, August 10, 1930.

*

President Hoover's square face and stiff
collars seem to have inspired artists to take
an Art Déco approach in caricaturing him.
Miguel Covarrubias and Charles Dunn created rather geometric and colorful versions
of Hoover's face, exaggerating his familiar
collar into a prominent, simple shape which
repeats the contours of the face. Similarly,
Paolo Garretto, an Italian caricaturist whose
work appeared in magazines of various
countries, created this particular abstract
and negative caricature of Hoover. The caption, probably added by the *World* editors,
points out the "high protective collar," playing on the controversy over a high protective tariff bill signed by Hoover in 1930. Although his hope was to stimulate business
as a remedy for the depression, the new
rates did more long range economic harm
than good.   A.H.

The President of the United States, Herbert Clark Hoover, Looking Ahead Over the Top of a High Protective Collar

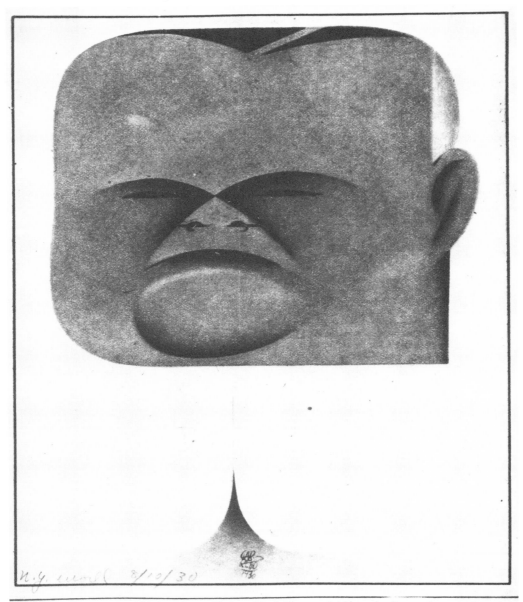

The President of the United States. Herbert Clark Hoover. looking ahead over the top of a high protective collar

1933-1961
Franklin D. Roosevelt to Dwight D. Eisenhower

Artist Unknown. [Untitled caricature of Franklin D. Roosevelt]. (n.d.). Graphite and watercolor on paper. 12 × 7". Collection Franklin D. Roosevelt Library, Hyde Park, New York.

*

Since the term of his distant cousin Theodore, Franklin Delano Roosevelt was probably the best Presidential subject to caricature. Artists quickly picked up on his pince-nez, the prominent chin and broad, urbane smile, the ever-present cigarette holder tilted at a jaunty angle. They tried to capture his confident attitude—his gesture of throwing back his head—and the impenetrable facade which antagonized some people, but which many others found to be highly reassuring. Roosevelt was so successful in imparting this air of control and assuredness that although he had been crippled for many years prior to his election, and though his health had deteriorated progressively during his last few years in office, he was always represented by cartoonists as a man of great vigor and health. He was never shown as physically disabled, for he carefully made sure that this impression was never conveyed to the American public.

In this fine example of a Rooseveltian caricature the anonymous artist has portrayed FDR with most of his usual attributes. Through minimal use of line, emphasis on the head, and exaggeration and elongation of the body, the cartoonist captures the essence of the Roosevelt style. Here is the image of a President who was to overshadow Congress in his more than twelve years in office, and who shaped the idea of the modern Presidency.   J.B.

UNTITLED CARICATURE OF FRANKLIN D. ROOSEVELT

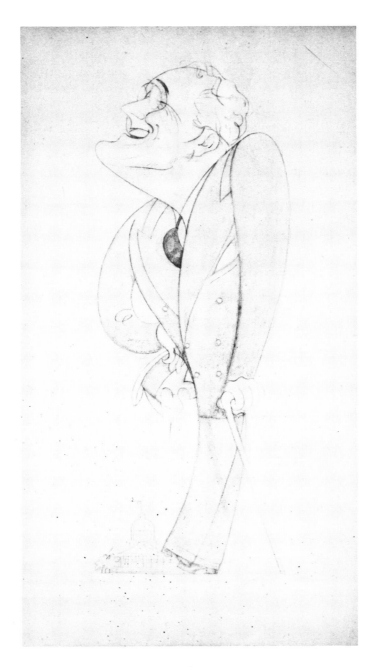

Peter Arno. [Untitled caricature of FDR and Hoover]. (Detail). (1933). Photomechanical color reproduction. 11⅞ × 8¾". Collection Franklin D. Roosevelt Library, Hyde Park, New York. Unpublished cover for March 4, 1933 issue of *The New Yorker*.

*

When in 1932 Franklin Delano Roosevelt became the Democratic Presidential nominee, he faced as his opposition the incumbent Republican President Herbert Hoover. The platforms of both parties were similar in many ways, and so the race was in actuality a campaign of personalities. Roosevelt, with his charismatic personality, showed great confidence and high spirit in his campaign. Hoover, grim and determined, gave long, dull speeches in defense of his much-criticized administration. Exchanges of charges and insults between the two contenders highlighted the campaign and continued until election day when Roosevelt won an overwhelming victory (taking all but six states) to become the thirty-second President of the United States.

In this cover drawing for *The New Yorker*, Peter Arno, the brilliant caricaturist, prophetically foresaw the events of the Inauguration drive that symbolized the end of Herbert Hoover's administration and the beginnings of the Roosevelt era. While a large crowd gapes and struggles to see the passing Presidents, Hoover ignores them, silently and sullenly glancing at FDR. Roosevelt has turned from his predecessor to acknowledge the cheering masses. In an extreme exaggeration of Roosevelt's constant grin, Arno has elongated FDR's teeth to draw further attention to their gleaming whiteness, and has stretched the enormous mouth over half of Roosevelt's face. The cover was predated, as are all magazines, and thus the drawing was created prior to the actual Inauguration Day. However, it corresponds exactly to what happened on March 4, 1933. Hoover refused to speak on the drive to the Capitol, and finally, Roosevelt, out of frustration, decided that "the two of us simply couldn't sit there on our hands ignoring each other and everyone else. So I began to wave..."

The drawing is representative of the sophisticated and witty style of Arno, whose cartoons were an artistic mainstay of *The New Yorker* for over forty years, until his death in 1968. Arno was a highly competent draftsman, always in perfect control of his economical line.

This drawing is a rare copy of the magazine cover, since it was never published. The editors decided to substitute a less topical cover for *The New Yorker* after the February 15, 1933 assassination attempt on Roosevelt, in which Mayor Anton Czermak of Chicago was killed while riding in a car. J.B.

UNTITLED CARICATURE OF FDR AND HOOVER

Miguel Covarrubias. "FDR Inauguration".
(1933). Photomechanical color reproduction.
21½ × 25⅞". Collection Franklin D. Roosevelt Library, Hyde Park, New York. Appeared in *Vanity Fair*, March 1933.

*

This fanciful interpretation of FDR's first
inauguration appeared in the March 1933
issue of *Vanity Fair*, a sophisticated magazine for the upper class which flourished in
the 1920s and 1930s. The drawing is the
work of Miguel Covarrubias, a noted Mexican caricaturist and illustrator, whose amusing, stylized depictions of the wealthy and
the famous appeared often in the pages of
Vanity Fair and *The New Yorker*. This
drawing is a take-off of the grand tradition
of David's *Coronation of Napoleon*, filled
with identifiable figures, given an imperial
setting of grandiose columns and drapery,
and opening out onto a scenic vista which
goes beyond the boundaries of Washington,
D.C. The divine royalty allusion is completed by the hovering angels announcing
the inauguration with trumpet blasts as
Chief Justice Charles Evans Hughes places
a wreath on FDR's head—the same symbol
of power which was worn by the Roman
Caesars and by Napoleon.

From the day Franklin D. Roosevelt won his
mandate to his inauguration four months
later, the country's economic ills continued
to decline. Industrial production had
dropped to an all-time low, while runs on
banks became evermore frequent. The
American people were desperate for leadership, and they listened carefully to the
words of what they hoped was the beginning of their New Deal. Roosevelt began
his first inaugural address by immediately
asserting his belief in the ability of America
to recover from economic ruin. He regarded
the Presidency as "a place of moral leadership" and asked Congress for broad powers
to fulfill the vacuum. "They have asked for
discipline and direction under leadership,"
the President replied to the Americans who
elected him. "They have made me the present instrument of their wishes. In the spirit
of the gift I take it ....May (God) guide me
in the days to come!"   J.B./M.M.

William Gropper. "Come Up and See Me
Sometime". (1934). Ink on paper. 17 ×
12½". Collection the artist.

*

"Come Up and See Me Sometime" is a delightful portrayal of FDR by William
Gropper. Though Roosevelt was seen in
many guises, Gropper's caricature of him
as Mae West is among the most original and
imaginative. One of the most popular movie
stars of the 1930s, Miss West was known for
her hourglass figure, extravagant wardrobe
and costly jewelry. Another Mae West characteristic was her unquestioned domination
of the men in her life. Gropper has used all
of Miss West's recognizable traits in his caricature of President Roosevelt, but it is this
last characteristic which he stressed. As seen
by the items on the table, we find that FDR
not only has the friendship of Wall Street,
big business, and the senators who seemed
sympathetic to these special groups, he is
the controlling party in these relationships.
The socialist belief in this period, expressed
by Gropper, was that Roosevelt was anti-
labor and had allied himself with the powerful moneyed interests in the country.
J.B./M.M.

COME UP AND SEE ME SOMETIME

David Low. "Fishing Talk". (1941). Photographic reproduction of the published version of the cartoon which appeared in *Years of Wrath/A Cartoon History: 1931-1945*, published by Simon and Schuster, Inc., 1946.

*

David Low's 1941 cartoon is an example of President Franklin Roosevelt's full assumption of Presidential powers. "Fishing Talk" is the cartoonist's light metaphor for the very serious conference held in 1941 by President Roosevelt and Prime Minister Churchill aboard the cruiser "Augusta." At a time when FDR was convinced America was destined to enter World War II, he could not as yet commit the nation to a full-scale effort due to the strong isolationist sentiment. Roosevelt nevertheless felt it was time to plan common strategies for the years of war and peace; the agreements concerning peace that arose from this conference were later presented to the world as the Atlantic Charter. The missing "Joe" in the picture is Joseph Stalin. Both Churchill and Roosevelt were sensitive to the place of the Soviet Union in the global panorama.

The British cartoonist, David Low, was a favorite of FDR's. A self-taught artist, Low was born in New Zealand and worked in Australia before going to England after World War I. In 1927 he joined the London *Evening Standard.* Although the paper was known for its right-wing policy, his cartoons often expressed an opposite point of view. And indeed, his graphic wit, his clarity of line and elimination of shading, made him the leading political cartoonist of an era.   J.B./M.M.

FISHING TALK

Clifford Berryman. "FDR Eclipses the Supreme Court". (1937). Ink over graphite on paper. 13½ × 14¼". Collection Library of Congress. Reproduced in the *Washington Star*, April 23, 1937.

*

The Constitutionally assigned powers of the President, the Congress and the Supreme Court have been at the heart of American politics from the earliest days of the Republic. Each branch of government has challenged the powers of the other two. The fundamental question has always been which is carrying out the "will of the people."

During Franklin D. Roosevelt's first term in office, much of the legislation passed by Congress at the President's urging was declared "unconstitutional" by the Supreme Court. Roosevelt believed that the Court was misreading the powers of the Congress and the President, and he presented a proposal to the Congress which would have increased the size of the Court and permitted him to appoint enough new members to approve the new legislation. Congress, however, refused to support his proposal. By this time, though, the majority of the Court had shifted and it began to approve the new legislation. Also, some members of the Court retired and some others died. Roosevelt was given the opportunity to appoint new members. The Constitutional crisis passed.

Clifford Berryman's cartoon clearly says, the President is blotting out the Court. However, when the skies cleared the Court was still there. The Congress and the President had changed their approach to many problems. Fundamental agreement had been reached on one of the classic political battles.   T.B.

FDR ECLIPSES THE SUPREME COURT

Leo Joseph Roche. "The Sphinx—1940 Model". (1940). Black and white crayon, pen and ink on paper. Plate dimensions, 16½ × 13½". Collection Franklin D. Roosevelt Library, Hyde Park, New York. Reproduced in the *Buffalo Courier-Express*, date unknown.

Daniel Fitzpatrick. "Next!" (1944). Photoengraving of the original drawing. 15 × 11½". Collection Harry S. Truman Presidential Library and Museum, Independence, Missouri. Appeared in the *St. Louis Post-Dispatch*, July 5, 1944.

*

Roosevelt's ever-present smile gave an inscrutable attitude to his political and public actions which often made it impossible for others to determine exactly what he was thinking. Throughout his Presidential career, the sphinx came to be a common symbol of his enigmatic personality, and was especially invoked on the issue of whether, in 1940, he would run for a third term in office. When FDR finally did decide to run, his decision was supposed to have been based on the crucial problem of the growing war in Europe; yet both President Roosevelt and Wendell Wilkie, the Republican nominee, conducted anti-war campaigns. On election day Roosevelt carried 38 states. It was the first time a man had been elected to the office of the President for a third term.

In Roche's cartoon Roosevelt/sphinx is shown in front of the Egyptian pyramids smoking away the unanswered third term question. His blank glasses and clenched teeth reinforce the mystery of the answer known only to Roosevelt. On the ground the little figures of Farley, Garner, McNutt, and Wheeler, all Democratic Presidential hopefuls for the 1940 campaign, gesture in frustration as they attempt to fathom Roosevelt's enigma—knowing that they will all be eliminated if Roosevelt decides to run again.

Four years later, Daniel Fitzpatrick's cartoon, "Next!", echoed Roche's feeling that Roosevelt had become the embodiment of the Democratic Party. By 1944, the year before the end of World War II, the President's popularity and power had become enormous. Not only had Roosevelt become a symbol in whom the American people could put their trust, he also held the confidence and esteem of the Allied countries. Again, there was no doubt that Roosevelt would become the Democratic Presidential nominee if he agreed to accept the nomination. Despite extremely poor health, Roosevelt accepted the nomination and was elected to serve a fourth unprecedented term.

Born in 1891, Daniel Fitzpatrick studied as a young man at the Art Institute of Chicago before going to work as the editorial cartoonist for Joseph Pulitzer's *St. Louis Post-Dispatch*. While working for the *Post-Dispatch* Fitzpatrick asserted his independence by expressing his own ideas in his cartoons, refusing to merely reflect the political viewpoint of the paper. His example has since been followed by many of today's editorial cartoonists.   J.B.

THE SPHINX—1940 MODEL / NEXT!

Courtesy, Buffalo Courier-Express.

Fitzpatrick in the St. Louis Post-Dispatch

William Gropper. "L'Etat C'est Moi".
(c. 1941). Ink and acetate on paper. 20 ×
14½". Collection the artist.

*

In "L'Etat C'est Moi" William Gropper drew
a direct correlation between FDR and Louis
XIV, the Sun King of France. Louis, who believed that he was king by divine right, is
the ultimate symbol of despotic power;
"L'Etat c'est moi" was his famous comment
on his connection to the government of
France—"I am the state." It was obviously
Gropper's fear that Roosevelt had assumed
this to be similarly true of his Presidency.
Like a formal portrait of Louis, Gropper
placed FDR in the elaborate dress of the
17th century, presenting a figure of formi-
dable power, force, and arrogance. The
drawing presents the inherent potential dangers of a man serving three terms in the
Presidency, a situation which carries with
it the implied threat of a possible dictator-
ship. In the 1930s Roosevelt had already assumed more powers than any President
before him, and at the time this cartoon was
executed, he was beginning to assume war
powers even before war had actually been
declared.

William Gropper, whose other mocking
satire of FDR also appears in this book (see
no. 74), was born in New York in 1897.
Growing up in a poor family, Gropper's
first-hand experiences of the hardships of
the poor made him sensitive to political
and social injustices. He has devoted much
of his long artistic career to sympathetically
presenting the life of the working people
and to harshly condemning the ruling economic class. After studying at the Ferrer
School (with Robert Henri and George
Bellows) and at the New York School of
Fine and Applied Arts, Gropper began a
popular and prolific career. His caricatures
have most often been found in radical journals, but his work has appeared in many
publications, ranging from *Vanity Fair* to
the socialist *New Masses*. In the mid-1930s
Gropper began to exhibit paintings, and his
accomplishments in that medium have long
been recognized.   J.B.

L'ETAT C'EST MOI

David Low. "A Fine Team—But Could Do with a Dash of Unity". (1945). Photographic reproduction of the published version of the cartoon which appeared in *Years of Wrath/A Cartoon History: 1931-1945*, published by Simon and Schuster, Inc., 1946.

*

The formation of the United Nations had been agreed to in 1945 by Churchill, Stalin and Roosevelt as part of the Yalta Agreement. While Roosevelt had been instrumental in persuading the United States and the Western world as to the necessity of such a peace-keeping organization, it was Truman, who, after Roosevelt's death, actually pressed forward to the establishment of the U.N. In doing so, Truman acted out the wishes of both Congress and the country, for Roosevelt had been extremely effective in his arguments.

British cartoonist David Low had his doubts about the success of an international organization based on cooperation when each of the four major victorious World War II allies seemed eager to control it. As the quote in the upper left-hand corner and the various uniforms imply, each world leader is ready to organize, according to his own country's interests, but does not seem willing to make any concessions to the other countries.   J.B.

A FINE TEAM—BUT COULD DO WITH A DASH OF UNITY

"A FINE TEAM—BUT COULD DO WITH A DASH OF UNITY..." .

Walt Kelly. "Whose Move?" (1946). Ink over graphite on paperboard. 12 × 10". Collection Harry S. Truman Library and Museum, Independence, Missouri.

*

In 1948, three years after the end of World War II, the United States and her allies decided that their occupation zones in Germany should receive a larger measure of self-government. Because of its expansionist drive to absorb European countries, the Soviet Union feared that the independence of West Germany would cause America to align itself with the new state permanently. This would not only consolidate America's influence in Europe, it would also block any further Soviet expansion to the West. Premier Stalin of the Soviet Union therefore ordered a blockade of the Allied occupied zone of West Berlin, a city surrounded by the Soviet controlled sector of East Germany.

"Whose Move?" is Walt Kelly's appraisal of the Berlin situation during this crisis. The question in the title appears to be rhetorical in this depiction of a chess game played by Truman and Stalin in which Berlin becomes the playing board. The careful, diplomatic moves of Cold War strategy have been upset by an unorthodox play by Stalin; his sitting on the board is symbolic of his sudden blockade of West Berlin. Truman seems unable to move, for Stalin has locked him into his chair (or position) by having placed his feet on the President's lap. Dressed in Russian peasant attire, Stalin is much larger than Truman. He confidently grins as he waits patiently for Truman to concede that the game is over. Yet even though seated in a seemingly impossible position, Truman does not appear ready to give up. His face is set and determined, and his hands grasp the arms of his chair in a preparatory fighting position. Though Stalin is on top, Truman is not to be underestimated.

President Truman handled this major international crisis superbly through his initiation of a massive air-lift over Berlin. His success in this situation was not an isolated victory, however, but a continuation of his successful opposition to Russia's western expansion.

The name of Walt Kelly appeared more often on the comic pages of newspapers than on the editorial page. He is best known as the creator of "Pogo," one of the few consistently political comic strips, in which Kelly used animal characters to express his liberal viewpoint.   J.B./M.M.

WHOSE MOVE?

Ben Shahn. "A Good Man is Hard to Find". (1948). Color lithograph. 43¾ × 29¾". Collection New Jersey State Museum: Gift of the New Jersey Junior and Community College Association. Published by the Progressive Party, New York City, 1948.

*

This 1948 campaign poster by Ben Shahn is a take-off of a famous 1945 photograph by Charles Cort which appeared in *Life* magazine. It showed Truman playing the piano with acresss Lauren Bacall reclining over it. Truman's piano playing was always the object of many jokes, but in this case, Shahn has brought Thomas Dewey, the Republican Presidential candidate, into the picture in order to make a derogatory comment on both. Truman is portrayed with mocking humor: his body is a lump except for the enlarged head and small feet; his frozen smile, blank glasses and one-handed playing make him appear almost lifeless. Dewey is not pictured as much better, as he's slung across the top of the piano in the pose of a cabaret singer. The inclusion of the word-image (e.g., "A Good Man is Hard to Find," "It Had to be You," and "Blest be the Tie that Binds") is typical of Shahn's work and is used as part of the satirical message.

Ben Shahn was born in Lithuania and immigrated to the United States with his family in 1906. He came from a family of craftsmen and continued in this tradition when he became an apprentice to a lithographer. He later studied at New York University, City College of New York, and the National Academy of Design. In the late 1920s, Shahn became politically radicalized and brought this new philosophy into his art. During the 1948 Presidential campaign, Shahn was a supporter of the Progressive Party, which had as its candidate former Vice-President Henry Wallace. This poster was published by the Progressive Party, New York City.

Another Shahn work appears in this book; see no. 86.   J.B.

A GOOD MAN IS HARD TO FIND

"Kukryniksy". "It Will Help the Way that Bandages Help a Dead Man" [English translation from the Russian]. (1949). Color offset-lithograph. Plate dimensions, 10¼ × 7½". Collection The General Library, University of California, Berkeley. Appeared in *Krokodil* (USSR), 1949.

*

Some of the best cartoons in the 1930s and 1940s came from the Soviet Union. An example of one of these is this 1949 cartoon, showing President Truman trying unsuccessfully to use American dollars as healing plasters on the body of Chiang Kai-shek, President of China and commander of the Chinese Nationalist Army. In full support of Chiang and his fight against the Communists, Truman had given massive financial aid and military arms to the weakened Nationalist forces. United States assistance, however, could not prevail over the incompetence of Chiang and his generals. The Nationalist forces continued to receive devastating losses from the Communists until 1949, when they retreated to the island of Formosa and continued their government from there.

The cartoon originally appeared in *Krokodil*, a Soviet humor magazine published by *Pravda*, the official newspaper of the Soviet Union. Since its inception shortly after the Bolshevik Revolution, *Krokodil* has continued to be a mouthpiece for Soviet policy.

During the late 1940s, the three main cartoonists of *Krokodil*—Kupriyanov, Drylov, and Nicholas Sokolov—working together under the portmanteau of "Kukryniksy," began personal attacks on President Truman. In this very unattractive depiction, the portrayal is accomplished through the use of bold lines and form and carefully rendered details. Truman is recognizable by his ratty hat, his glasses and sharp nose. The cartoon uses brilliant contrasting colors to achieve a poster-like effect.   J.B./M.M.

It Will Help the Way that Bandages Help a Dead Man

Herbert Block (Herblock). "If There's Anything I Hate it's Sloppy Neighbors". (1951).
Ink and graphite on paper. 16½ × 12". Collection the artist. Reproduced in the *Washington Post*, December 21, 1951.

*

During Truman's Presidency, numerous
scandals arose involving some White House
officials and employees of several executive
departments. Though he was pressured by
Congress to do so, the President usually
refused to accept the various charges because of his faith in the integrity of his staff.
Congress was, however, powerful enough to
eventually force the President to submit,
and during the early 1950s Congressional
investigations of wrongdoing in the executive branch took place. The irony of the
situation was that many members of Congress were themselves subject to attack for
acceptance of political contributions in return for official favors.

"If There's Anything I Hate it's Sloppy
Neighbors" is Herblock's view of these investigations. As is usual in a Herblock cartoon, Congress is represented by a fat, bald-
ing man with glasses. Congress ignores his
own messy backyard and sloppy appearance as he leans over the fence to criticize
his next-door neighbor, President Truman.
The President looks upset, yet resolute, as
he attempts to clean up the dirty laundry
of his executive departments. Note that
Truman himself wears totally clean clothes,
Block's comment on the President's personal morality and ethical standards.
J.B./M.M.

IF THERE'S ANYTHING I HATE IT'S SLOPPY NEIGHBORS

Herblock copyright cartoon, 1951

David Levine. "Truman with Hat". 1974.
Ink on paper. 13¾ × 11". Courtesy Forum
Gallery, New York City. Reproduced in *The
New York Review of Books*, 1974.

*

Harry S. Truman was subject to much
heavy criticism during his terms as President. A broad segment of the population
and many news commentators gave only
hesitant approval to his policies. In foreign
affairs, for example, issues such as the following were debated: How should the United States deal with the U.S.S.R. in regard
to Europe? The Middle East? Should the
United States intervene in Korea? Should
MacArthur be dismissed? How should the
U.S. deal with the People's Republic of
China?

This David Levine caricature was produced
in *The New York Review of Books* to ac-
company Murray Kempton's reviews of
Merrill Miller's *Speaking Frankly* and J. K.
Blum's editing of *H. A. Wallace's Diary
(1942-1946)*. It answers none of the above
questions, but says, "Here he is; you be the
judge." It is not intended to be a likeness of
Truman, but rather implies a man who is
tough (note the boxing gloves), frank, open,
radiating the feeling, "Here-I-am-doing-the-
best-I-can-under-circumstances-not-of-my-
choosing."   T.B.

TRUMAN WITH HAT

Ben Shahn. "Watch Out for the Man on a White Horse!" (1952). Offset-lithograph. 14⁷⁄₁₆ × 10". Collection New Jersey State Museum: Gift of Bernarda Bryson Shahn. Published by Volunteers for Stevenson, Roosevelt, New Jersey, 1952.

*

Eisenhower's great personal charm (his popularity with the troops he commanded was enormous), his famous smile and his seemingly easy-going nature made most Americans forget the traditional warning about the "man on a white horse." But Eisenhower's candidacy for President in 1952 was looked upon with apprehension by Ben Shahn, who made this anti-Eisenhower campaign poster into a warning to the American populace. Gone is the humor associated with Shahn's poster of Truman and Dewey from the 1948 campaign (see no. 82); this caricature is biting and satirical. Shahn did not want the American public to forget that as General of the Armies Eisenhower had had great authority in the army—possibly too much authority for a potential President.
J.B./M.M.

Herbert Block (Herblock). "Have a Care, Sir". (1954). Ink and graphite on paper. 16½ ×12". Collection the artist. Reproduced in the *Washington Post*, March 4, 1954.

*

In an era which was known for acts of complicity and silence due to fear, cartoonist Herblock put on a courageous fight against Senator Joseph McCarthy and the similarly biased investigations of the House Un-American Activities Committee, which, since the 1930s, had functioned under the Chairmanship of Martin Dies. Herblock was appalled by the hysterical anti-Communist movement of the early 1950s and coined the term "McCarthyism" to denote its major proponent. In his many protest drawings of this period, Herblock may have been the strongest crusading cartoonist since the days of Thomas Nast's attacks on Boss Tweed and Tammany Hall.

McCarthy had gained much of his popularity as one of numerous anti-Communist crusaders during the Truman administration. President Eisenhower disliked the questionable tactics McCarthy used in his role as Chairman of the Senate Permanent Investigations Subcommittee, but did little to restrain him. Eisenhower publicly stated that as McCarthy was a senator, his own peers would have to deal with him, since he himself had no jurisdiction over the Senate.

Herblock saw Eisenhower's position as ineffectual, to say the least, and expressed his feelings in "Have a Care, Sir". The message of the cartoon is carried out through the simplicity of the composition which consists almost entirely of the two figures standing in opposition in the two halves of the drawing. Ike is seen ludicrously threatening the hatchet-wielding Wisconsin Senator with a feather for his weapon. Whereas Eisenhower is depicted with an air of incredulousness, Herblock reserves his greater contempt for McCarthy, portraying him with an evil and menacing sneer. His hairy hands and deeply shadowed, unshaven face, and his hulking stance give McCarthy an almost ape-like appearance.   J.B./T.B.

"HAVE A CARE, SIR"

HERBLOCK
©1959 THE WASHINGTON POST CO.

Cy Hungerford. "A Presidential Touch". (1957). Pen and ink on paper. 16½ × 13⅛". Collection Dwight D. Eisenhower Presidential Library. Reproduced in the *Pittsburgh Post Gazette, c. 1957.*

*

"Brother, can you spare about 72 million dollars?" the panhandler President asks Congress. The rotund "mark" looks astounded, and with good reason: a chief executive known for his determination to cut the budget has asked for more money than any President in history up to that time.

In spending—as in legislation—Eisenhower discovered that the President has only the most limited of influences. Intending to reduce federal costs, he balked at federal aid to housing and education. Year by year, however, the budget rose, and with it the deficit, as well. The fact was, some things could not be cut: without military spending and foreign aid the nation's posture in foreign affairs would be weakened, and without domestic outlays, the economy of the country would go into a sharp decline.

After 1958, however, the President found the weapon to keep down spending in his use of the veto power. He vetoed two public housing measures, two anti-recession public works bills, an area redevelopment proposal, and anti-pollution legislation. Though Congress expanded social security and raised both minimum wages and unemployment compensation, it could not challenge the veto, and the result was two years of stalemate after six years of drift. The Congress elected in 1958 had been strongly Democratic; thanks to Eisenhower's obstructiveness, it did little more than its more conservative predecessor. Some Presidents are known for what they have done; Eisenhower will be remembered for what he did not do, and how diligently he kept things from being done.

Cy Hungerford's style is extremely simple. Determined to let the ideas stand unaided by artistic fillips, he began to cartoon in simple blacks and whites in the era of William Howard Taft—when a good cartoon had thousands of crosshatched lines and caricatures screamed with copious detail. For more than fifty years he continued to draw in quick, rounded brush lines and with pleasant humor. In contrast to most of the great figures in the profession, Hungerford kept his work free of viciousness. But the price of gentleness is a high one: the cartoons never had much political impact because they never outraged anyone, and the innocence retained in the cartoons robbed them of much of the artistic power they might otherwise have had.   M.S.

A PRESIDENTIAL TOUCH

Herbert Block (Herblock). "Don't Get Hysterical—I'm Watching All the Time". (1958). Ink and graphite on paper. 16½ × 12". Collection the artist. Reproduced in the *Washington Post*, April 24, 1958.

*

Herbert Block (Herblock). "And All This Time I Was Hoping You'd Speak Up". (1958). Ink and graphite on paper. 16½ × 12". Collection the artist. Reproduced in the *Washington Post*, August 28, 1958.

*

As military leader, particularly in his relations with political and military figures in Europe, Dwight Eisenhower showed much skill in his ability to make essential decisions and to deal with important issues. But as President, Eisenhower never really mastered the political and economic leadership which the office demanded. In "Don't Get Hysterical—I'm Watching All the Time," Herblock reflects this low-keyed Presidency. Faced with a recession in early 1958, Eisenhower received advice from many directions as to what should be done. With many conflicting opinions, it is not surprising that he was hesitant to make any move. But it was characteristic of his Presidency that by the middle of his second term he had not yet acquired the firm touch needed to face the problem. In the midst of foreign difficulties and domestic strikes, as well as the recession, he was still "watching."

A few months later, Herblock commented again on Eisenhower's lack of action. He used the image of the sphinx to comment on the President's long-awaited statement on the desegregation issue of the 1950s, as his silence matched that of the fabled Egyptian sphinx. The cobwebs attached to Eisenhower indicate the length of time that had passed since the Supreme Court decision on segregation on May 17, 1954. For four and a half years the President was silent on this very significant issue, giving none of what Block called "moral leadership" to the country. At a White House press conference on August 27, 1958, the President finally declared that he thought desegregation in the United States should go at a slower rate. Uncle Sam reacts in astonishment to this news as the grim-faced Eisenhower waves a traffic sign announcing his attitude.

By hesitating to use the power of his office to enforce the ruling of *Brown vs. Topeka*, Eisenhower left the fate of desegregation to the individual states. Although he managed to assuage the feelings of his Southern supporters, he stimulated a widespread reaction of outrage among many black and white national leaders. The lack of a sense of urgency in his desegregation policies led to the civil rights crisis in the following decade. J.B./T.B.

DON'T GET HYSTERICAL—I'M WATCHING ALL THE TIME / AND ALL THIS TIME I WAS HOPING YOU'D SPEAK UP

Bill Mauldin. "Just Between Us Fellows, Who Was at the Controls?" (1960). Ink and black crayon on paper. 15⅛ × 11¼". Collection Library of Congress. Reproduced in the *St. Louis Post-Dispatch*, 1960.

*

President Eisenhower and Nikita Krushchev struggled many times to achieve some form of detente, yet it seemed that every favorable move by one was offset by a negative move of the other. Just when the two leaders were scheduled to meet in Europe, an American plane was downed over central Russia. After several attempts to cover up what had happened, it became known that the pilot had been captured and much of the plane salvaged. It was a CIA U2.

President Eisenhower assumed full responsibility for the affair, and Krushchev cancelled the proposed meeting. Many questions concerning the flight began to arise: Why did the plane fly at that critical time? Why did the plane fly at all? Exactly how much control did Eisenhower actually have over the flight? Yet perhaps more important, the question arose as to how much control a President should have over the many thousands of details operating in international affairs. If, for example, the President makes the general decision that we will fly over Russia, yet leaves it up to others to determine when the flights will take place, is he responsible for the unfortunate decision of others? These questions remain unanswered, and as the plane is seen vaguely on the horizon, President Eisenhower and Secretary of State Dulles are asking, "Who was at the controls?"   T.B.

JUST BETWEEN US FELLOWS, WHO WAS AT THE CONTROLS?

"JUST BETWEEN US, FELLOWS, WHO WAS AT THE CONTROLS?"

Hugh Haynie. "Kennedy Contemplating the Bust of McCormack". 1961. Pencil, black ink and gouache on paper. 19 × 14¼". Collection The Metropolitan Museum of Art: Gift of Pierre Salinger, 62: 527. Reproduced in the Louisville *Courier-Journal*, 1961.

*

Though powerful in foreign affairs, John Kennedy's Presidency was characterized by his inability to successfully deal with Congress. Cartoonist Hugh Haynie captures Kennedy's frustration in his satire of *Aristotle Contemplating the Bust of Homer*, in which the President examines the bust of Speaker of the House, John McCormack.

On Capitol Hill, a coalition of Republicans and Southern Democrats consistently voted down Kennedy's measures, conservative chairmen stifled proposals in their committees, and the leaders of both branches proved uncooperative. In 1960, Lyndon Johnson manipulated and pressured the Senate to legislative ends; Sam Rayburn did the same as Speaker of the House. A year later, Rayburn had retired and Johnson was restless in the impotency of the vice presidency. Their successors lacked enthusiasm either for liberal reform or for armtwisting. As a result, a bill for general aid to elementary and secondary education died, as did proposals to create a Department of Urban Affairs, a Federal Advisory Council on the Arts, and a Medicare plan. A public works program passed the Senate by one vote; a farm bill lost in the House by five votes. Though many bills did pass, they were all in watered-down form. By late 1963, a host of vital measures ranging from a tax cut to a civil rights bill stagnated in Congress with little prospect of passage. M.S.

KENNEDY CONTEMPLATING THE BUST OF MCCORMACK

Kennedy Contemplating The Bust Of McCormack

FOR PIERRE SALINGER —
WITH MANY THANKS

Herbert Block (Herblock). "Let's Get a Lock
for this Thing". (1962). Ink and graphite
on paper. 16½ × 12". Collection the artist.
Reproduced in the *Washington Post*, November 1, 1962.

*

In "Let's Get a Lock for this Thing" Herblock
deals with one of his frequent topics, the
threat of nuclear war. With a paradoxical
spirit of togetherness during the time of their
most serious confrontation, both Krushchev
and Kennedy struggle to contain the danger
that the Cuban Missile Crisis came so close
to setting free. Instead of treating the Soviet
leader as a villain, the cartoonist depicts
him as fairly as the President, and demonstrates that the nuclear peril is a danger to
all men.   M.S.

"LET'S GET A LOCK FOR THIS THING"

Herblock copyright cartoon, 1962

Jules Feiffer. "The Frontier Drag". (1963). Ink on paper. 11 × 21". Collection the artist. Reproduced in the *Village Voice*, May 26, 1963.

THE FRONTIER DRAG

Bill Mauldin. "Statue of Lincoln Weeping for Kennedy". (1963). Ink on paper. 16½ × 13". Collection John F. Kennedy Presidential Library. Reproduced in the *Chicago Sun-Times*, November 23, 1963.

STATUE OF LINCOLN WEEPING FOR KENNEDY

Robert Pryor. "Eggheads". (1972). Ink on paper. Two drawings: JFK, 4 × 9¾"; LBJ, 4¼ × 13". Collection Mr. and Mrs. Frederick Rudolph, Williamstown, Massachusetts. Reproduced in *The New York Times Book Review*, November 12, 1972.

*

One of the most noticeable features of Pryor's work is his presentation of human relationships in contrasting styles, and this highly amusing, two-part cartoon illustrates the point. In the top frame, the "eggheads"—Kennedy's cabinet and special advisors, Theodore Sorensen, Robert McNamara, Dean Rusk, Arthur Schlesinger, Jr.—rest comfortably in President Kennedy's firm hands. The second frame presents a broken carton held by a rough President Johnson, who is saddened by his cracked, messy unusable acquisition. This pair of drawings summarizes the carefully selected Kennedy cabinet being transferred to Johnson. Although most of the cabinet members remained with Johnson, the group's identity was lost beyond repair.

The Pryor cartoon contrasts the two Presidents. If Kennedy was knight errant, perhaps Don Quixote, Johnson was Sancho Panza—Texas style. The personalities of these two men differed sharply, and their grasp of politics was also different. The political combine of the two, arranged in 1960 for the sake of a balanced Presidential ticket, lost its balance with Kennedy's assassination. Assuming the office of President is difficult under any circumstances, but for Johnson to do so under such ghastly circumstances was tragic. Yet Johnson's appeal for continuity was most persuasive. Retaining Kennedy's cabinet, urging Congressional passage of Kennedy's legislation and the formation of the Warren Commission, were

the acts of a statesman, as well as a skilled politician. During the period of transition Johnson was able to strengthen his powerful national image. And as history has shown, although he could not interact well with Kennedy's cabinet, he proved to be more skillful than his predecessor in his relationship with Congress.

Pryor is one of a group of New York-based artists whose work supplements political analysis in various journals. This cartoon was published as an illustration accompanying a review of *The Best and the Brightest* by David Halberstam. Pryor's work has appeared in *Harper's*, *Time*, *Psychology Today*, *Saturday Review*, and *The New York Times*.   M.M./J.P.

EGGHEADS

Pat Oliphant. "By Golly, Ky, the Natives
are Restless Tonight!" (1966). Ink on water-
sensitive paper. 11⅞ × 17⁹⁄₁₆". Collection
Lyndon Baines Johnson Presidential Library.
Reproduced in the *Denver Post*, February
13, 1966.

*

Nyugen Kao Ky was one of several to serve
as President of South Vietnam during the
time the United States was involved in that
country's war. Like President Lyndon Johnson, Ky faced great opposition—within his
own country—to his policies. In the cartoon, spears fly as President Johnson comments to his fellow President that they both
have troubles; for both heads of colonial
governments are bothered by the annoyance
of the "natives."   T.B.

By Golly, Ky, the Natives are Restless Tonight!

'BY GOLLY, KY, THE NATIVES ARE RESTLESS TONIGHT!'

Herbert Block (Herblock). "Ev Tu?" (1966).
Ink and graphite on paper. 16½ × 12". Collection the artist. Reproduced in the *Washington Post*, June 10, 1966.

*

For Lyndon Johnson, the Presidency symbolized the achievement of a life-long quest; and he used his office to secure what he believed would be of the greatest help to his fellow citizens. As he saw it, the war in Vietnam was fought to prevent the spread of Communism. Yet Americans, including his party, rejected what he felt was the most important use of his high office.

Herblock has used a classic device among cartoonists by showing President Johnson as Julius Caesar; and he quotes from the famous scene in Shakespeare's *Julius Caesar* when Brutus, Caesar's close friend, betrays him. In the cartoon, one of Johnson's aides, Bill Moyers, presents a scroll which tells the President that one of his oldest and closest associates in the Senate — Senator Everett Dirksen — has now indicated a loss of confidence with regard to the President's position on Vietnam. It is more than Johnson can bear, and the cartoonist allows himself the privilege of a double pun: "Ev Tu?"
T.B.

"EV TU?"

DIRKSEN ACCUSES ADMINISTRATION OF LACK OF CANDOR ON VIETNAM

Herblock copyright cartoon, 1966

©1966 HERBLOCK
THE WASHINGTON POST

Paul Szep. "A Senator Fulbright to See You,
Sire. Seems He Can't Reconcile Himself to
Your Infallibility". (1967). India ink on il-
lustration board. Reproduced in the *Boston
Globe*, March 1967.

*

In 1964—with only two senators dissent-
ing—Congress had passed the Gulf of Ton-
kin resolution, giving President Johnson the
right to act as he thought wise in Vietnam.
In return, Johnson habitually consulted
leading members of Congress, not neces-
sarily to obtain their consent or advice on
measures he was considering, but to secure
their acquiescence to measures he had already taken. By 1966, however, this good
will between Johnson and Congress had
faded. Senators including Fulbright began
to conduct investigations, and by 1967 were
in open opposition to the President.

More than any other newspaper satirist,
Paul Szep puts the soul of his targets in
their faces; thus all the arrogance and false-
ness he saw in Lyndon Johnson can be seen
between the brows and the chin. As Szep's
imperial ruler listens, a messenger crawls
up the steps with a note from the small and
distant chairman of the Senate Foreign Relations Committee, J. W. Fulbright. Clearly,
the cartoonist agrees with the Senator that
something is amiss when the President of
a democracy has turned into a combination
of pope and king, irreproachable and un-
approachable.   M.S.

'A Senator Fulbright to See You, Sire. Seems He Can't Reconcile Himself to Your Infallibility.'

Courtesy of the Boston Globe.

Paul Szep. "Unity". (1968). Ink and wash on paper. 11¾ × 14". Collection the artist. Reproduced in the *Boston Globe*, c. March 30, 1968.

*

On March 29, 1968, while addressing the nation on Vietnam, Lyndon Baines Johnson ended his speech by disclosing that he would not seek reelection. The cartoon suggests the impact of that announcement on Johnson's political life. Attired in the ritualistic hara-kiri costume, Johnson hunches forward in anticipation; the heavy texturing of the image indicates despair. A line is drawn from the centralized curvature of the spine and head to the taut handle of the double-edged sword; it then follows the blade to the point of the fatal impact. If Johnson's agonized features find repose it will only be through the thrust of the steel. There is no alternative or escape. The President is portrayed as a man who is longing for peace; his political life is ending.

At the beginning of his Presidency, Johnson brought unity to the nation at a time of strife and sorrow. Later he instigated a large legislative program and presided over unprecedented economic prosperity. Yet all of this was lost in the hostilities of the Vietnam dilemma, as Johnson could provide no resolution to the conflict either at home or abroad. At the time of his renunciation of future office he expressed a concern for unity reminiscent of his early Presidency. Johnson had hoped to be a unifying symbol not only of the American people but also of his party; in March 1968 he was neither of these. The Democratic Party was in open rebellion; primary elections had brought victories to both Eugene McCarthy and Robert Kennedy. Election politics would be bitter and Johnson sought to avoid another

battle. He commented at the time of his withdrawal from candidacy: "I am a free man, an American, a public servant and a member of my party—in that order, always and only."

In another Szep cartoon, "A Senator Fulbright to See You, Sire" (no. 99), Johnson's face reflects a man who is both sly and devious: his nose has become an ungainly beak, his mouth, a snarl. The eyes are only half-open, yet one senses that little passes by without his notice. Although the same facial elements are exaggerated in "Unity," the overall effect is radically different. Though Johnson's nose is still prominent there is nothing sinister about it. The closed eyes and the set of the mouth reflect an impression of humility, determination and benign acceptance. In this later cartoon, Szep forcefully conveys the magnanimous depth of Johnson's gesture.   J.P.

Courtesy of the Boston Globe

The Boston Globe

Paul Conrad. "Speaking of Sanctuaries..."
1970. Pen and ink on paper. 14 × 11⅟₁₆".
Collection the artist. Reproduced in the *Los Angeles Times*, May 1970.

*

The invasion of Cambodia, ordered by President Richard Nixon in 1970, was done swiftly and in characteristic secrecy—the purpose was to destroy Communist sanctuaries on Cambodian soil. The action was also meant to demonstrate the effectiveness of Nixon's "Vietnamization" plan. The mission was not a success, nor was it widely supported at home. According to opinion polls, the majority of the American public felt that the action should not be repeated and that the President had not been completely honest in his accounting of the affair.

"Speaking of Sanctuaries" comments on this Presidential order. The use of the Presidential seal is interesting since it not only dominates the cartoon but shields the man who is responsible for its use. Conrad uses the seal to signify the zenith of American power; the arrogant hands which move behind the symbol of power are Nixon's. The shield protects not only the questionable Cambodian activities, but the man responsible for them.

Winner of the Pulitzer Prize for his powerful and astute cartoons, Conrad's statements are as strong as the bold lines of his style. He began his cartooning career with the *Denver Post* before moving to the *Los Angeles Times*. As resident cartoonist for the *Times* he has complete control over the content of his cartoons, despite possible differences of opinion with the editorial staff.   J.P.

SPEAKING OF SANCTUARIES....

Edward Sorel. "Nixon as Quaker". (1970). Ink on paper. 11½ × 10¼". Collection the artist. Reproduced in the *Philadelphia Inquirer*, 1970.

*

This cartoon, a satire of the Quaker Oats symbol, is one of a series of "Pass the Lord and Praise the Ammunition" drawings by Edward Sorel. Each of them is a vivid condemnation of organized religion for its unquestioning support of the state. Specifically, this portrait reveals the contradictions between Nixon's Quaker heritage and his position as commander-in-chief during the Southeast Asian war. It also reveals the irony of a religion representing humility exemplified by a man named "Churchman of the Year" by the Religious Heritage Foundation of America.   J.P.

NIXON AS QUAKER

With apologies to Quaker Oats
and the Society of Friends

Edward Sorel

Robert Pryor. "Great Leap Forward".
(1972). Charcoal and graphite on paper.
11 × 8⅜". Collection the artist. Unpublished.

*

Nixon's trip to the Republic of China is the
theme of this Pryor cartoon. In it the artist has abandoned his usual pen and ink
technique in favor of charcoal pencil, resulting in a softer texture more in keeping
with the nature of what the artist is depicting—the soft, wet skins of frogs. Nixon's
"great leap forward" in world diplomacy is
playfully pictured in this literal image as
an awkward game of leap-frog rather than
as an accomplishment requiring great skill
and poise. The amphibian caricatures of
Mao and Nixon are strikingly effective and
highly amusing because their features seem
to adapt with ease to the appearance of
frogs. The oriental simplification and flat-
tening of the composition is entirely appropriate to the theme. Mao sits poised like a
serene jade figure while Nixon leaps toward
the great unknown.   J.P./M.M.

GREAT LEAP FORWARD

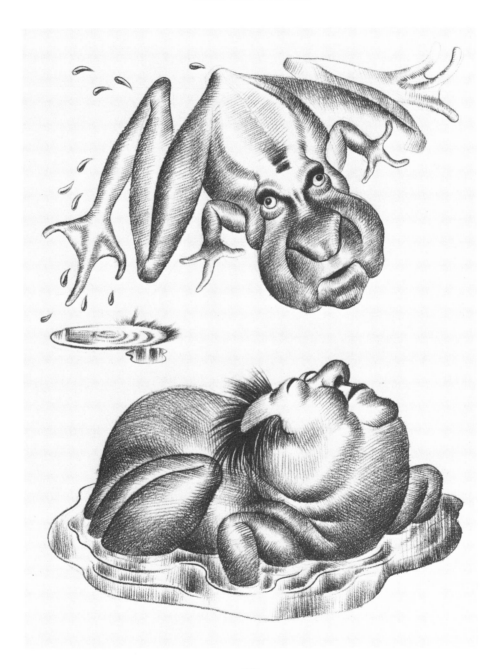

Robert Grossman, "Pinocchio and Jiminy Cricket". (1972). Tempera airbrushed on paper. 16 × 26". Collection the artist. Reproduced in the *National Lampoon*, date unknown.

*

Pinocchio and his friend, Jiminy Cricket, are appropriated from the storybook-movie to serve as caricature for a Nixon-Kissinger cartoon. Pinocchio is known as the little puppet whose nose grew in length every time he told a lie. Here, Grossman—playing with the familiar target of Nixon's nose—has exaggerated it to unparalled proportions. Kissinger, on the other hand, is reduced to the size of the Walt Disney cricket. Dressed for diplomatic travel, the small-bodied creature is reporting the information gathered on his mysterious wanderings to the young Pinocchio. The Nixon-Kissinger transformation pokes fun at the "advisor's" intimacy with his friend. It humorously suggests that detente is a team effort, yet it questions who directs whom.   J.P.

PINOCCHIO AND JIMINY CRICKET

Edward Sorel. "Nixon Crossing the Delaware". 1972. Ink on paper. 15½ × 23". Collection Ira. D. Rothfeld, M.D., New York, New York. Reproduced in the *Saturday Review*, July 1, 1972.

*

A "Second American Revolution" was the proposal President Nixon made in his 1971 State of the Union address. Edward Sorel translates that suggestion into a parody of the famous painting of *Washington Crossing the Delaware* by Emmanuel Leutze. Rather than a picturesque scene of triumph, however, Nixon is depicted on a sinking ship surrounded by figures who represent the opposing factions in contemporary American society. Nixon—in command—seems oblivious to the utter chaos around him, and everyone else is much too busy with his own fighting to notice that the ship is sinking. This comment on a contemporary political situation is in humorous contrast with the original painting of America's brave, heroic forefathers.

The 1971 State of the Union message was more than a verbal gesture aimed at reconciling American society. The "Second American Revolution" was to be the program by which Nixon hoped to establish a domestic policy and create a legislative record for the 1972 Presidential campaign. The Nixon administration had been accused of lacking direction and failing to give his domestic programs the necessary Congressional support that had characterized Lyndon Johnson's career. The program, also referred to as the "Big Six," would give Nixon a framework whereby he could modify the still unabsorbed Great Society legislation to more modest Republican proportions. This condensation of the federal bureaucracy is illustrated by the proposal for revenue sharing with local governments, described as a reform to "return power to the people." The program was to re-channel Great Society funds into new, undesignated, economic assistance which would be spent as decided upon by local officials. Such rhetorical proposals, whether substantiated or not, would generate popular approval and provide the legislative program for continuing the Nixon Presidency.

"Nixon Crossing the Delaware" is done in pen and ink highlighted with watercolor wash. It is drawn in a sketchy technique, almost like refined scribbling. Sorel reverses the usual comic style of using disproportionally large heads on small bodies, drawing instead monumental, bulky bodies with tiny heads and bulging eyes. The quick movement of Sorel's design emphasizes the action aboard ship and in the water below. J.P./M.M.

Andy Warhol. "Portrait of Nixon (Vote McGovern)". (1972). Color photo-silkscreen. 42⅛ × 42". Collection University Art Museum, Berkeley.

*

An erstwhile illustrator of ladies' shoes, a former window display man, painter, film-maker and the superstar of his own personal myth, Andy Warhol has created a new kind of political image, which does not fit into the old categories of cartoon and caricature. The most famous of the group of Pop artists who burst forth with great publicity in the early 1960s, Andy Warhol painted Campbell Soup cans and famous personalities with equal interest and detachment. He made portraits of our culture heroes, magnetic personalities and the "Beautiful People" such as Jacqueline Kennedy, Marilyn Monroe, Elizabeth Taylor, Mao Tse-tung, and —in this poster—Richard Nixon. It is interesting to note that Warhol has often selected the personalities for his pictures at specific critical times: Marilyn Monroe immediately after her suicide, Jacqueline Kennedy after the President's assassination, Richard Nixon during the questionable electoral campaign of 1972, conducted by the Committee to Re-Elect the President (CREEP).

The factor of immediate recognition is important in these mechanized portraits. They are standard, ready-made images and are representative of the work and place of the artist in the post-industrial age. Warhol has all his work done mechanically at "The Factory." He generally does not touch the work in its process from photograph to a silk screen to the stencilled painting and finally to a poster; yet it bears the unmistakable stamp of his authority. His selection of the particular photograph to be used and his decision to have the face placed in a frontal pose in the center of the straightforward composition gives his portraits a standardized look. He asks no questions.

Warhol destroys the stereotyped images and makes them grotesque through the use of color. He has, in a way, broken with the tradition in caricature which has always relied almost solely on line. In his "Portrait of Nixon" the President's face is bluish-green, set against a brushed-in yellow background and placed on top of a pink coat. The mouth, or rather the vacuous stage grin, is yellow. The garish and lurid colors, and the fact that they are smudged and largely out of register, give the grotesque quality to the picture. We are confronted with a face which is at once bland, impersonal, widely known, popular, but also enigmatic and rather monstrous. The message "Vote McGovern" results almost naturally from this image of his opponent.

An artist who has made a point of being non-committal, secretive and very detached, Warhol took a rare political stand in this poster which he contributed to the Democratic campaign in 1972. He represented Richard M. Nixon with a new kind of grotesquerie, which may add significantly to the development of the political caricature, and which is part of a new and sophisticated popular imagery of the sixties and seventies. P.S.

Ranan Lurie. [Caricature of Nixon with wheat]. (1973). Ink on paper. 13¼ × 11". Collection the artist. Syndicated by the Los Angeles Times Syndicate and the New York Times Syndicate, June 20, 1973.

*

In the initiation of foreign policy, the Nixon administration seemed to repudiate all the doctrines of Richard Nixon up to 1968. In contrast to his hard line policy in earlier years, the President attempted a détente with both Russia and Communist China, and did so with little or no help from Congress. The ability to sell wheat to both provides a marvelous balancing pole for his tight-rope walking.

Ranan Lurie's cartoon makes a simple pun, in a simple style, on Nixon's "summit conferences" in Peking and Moscow. But the cartoon also has complex connotations about the delicacies of Nixon's diplomatic tasks and his waverings in their execution. M.S.

CARICATURE OF NIXON WITH WHEAT

Robert Pryor. [Caricature of Nixon and members of Congress]. (c. 1973). Ink on paper. 13¹⁄₁₆ × 7½". Collection the artist. Reproduced in *Harper's* magazine, date unknown.

*

All of the essentials in Robert Pryor's work are present in this cartoon. The most striking characteristic is the imaginative, oblique arrangement of the composition. The idea of depicting Senate leaders hanging from Nixon's reins is made more comical by the way the figures are positioned within the cartoon. A determined Nixon appears as if seen from below. His stubborn chin and jowls jut forward and the remarkable nose is silhouetted in profile. In contrast to the "stubborn mule" depiction of the President are the playfully curving reins and the puny senators dangling from them.

The cartoon suggests the powerlessness of the Senate leaders to "bring to rein" the executive branch of government, a problem which reached the point of open confrontation in Nixon's second term. Nixon's attempt to rule "ex officio" was met with open hostility and concrete action. The more influential Senate leaders, as illustrated— Edward Kennedy, Hugh Scott, Mike Mansfield, Sam Ervin and Hubert Humphrey— began to test their ability to challenge Presidential actions. Their momentary lack of strength is well portrayed.

An example of the irritation which the senators suffered in the erosion of their power was the Presidential use of "executive agreements" in foreign affairs rather than treaties, which must be approved by the Senate. This practice had become quite common even before Nixon became President, and in 1973 the Senate and House of Representatives both began to limit the President's powers by resolution, legislation and restrictions on appropriations. However, the capacity of the President to act still remained powerful.

Robert Pryor uses cross-hatched lines of pen and ink in place of contours to outline his forms.   J.P.

By Edward Sorel for *New York Magazine*

David Levine. "Gerald Ford". 1974. Ink on paper. 13¾ × 11". Courtesy Forum Gallery, New York, New York. Reproduced in *The New York Review of Books*, 1974.

*

Many modern cartoonists seize on a distinguishing feature of a political figure and accentuate it to produce a powerful and instantly recognizable image. Other artists rely more on subtle and refined drawing. Levine's caricatures fall into the second category: he catches the character of his subject by the sensitive delineation of the facial expression. This technique is evident in this portrait of Gerald Ford and is also illustrated in Levine's drawing of President Truman (see no. 85).

President Ford's features do not lend themselves readily to either caricature or cartoon. Neither has his career been characterized by activities which can be easily distinguished. His early actions as President demonstrated his lack of interest in continuing the "Imperial Presidency" of Richard Nixon. On the contrary, leadership under Ford's administration moved to the Congress. The President's principle of "The less government the better," was represented by his attempts to prevent Congress from doing too much, and his vetoes limited the Congress' domination of the political direction. In this regard he continued to act as he did when he was Minority Leader in the House of Representatives. Such actions as were taken were forced by the flow of events, rather than through Ford's leadership. His leading officials—Kissinger, Schlesinger, Rumsfeld, Simon, Butz and Levy—showed great independence. The question was often, "Is the President supporting them?" rather than, "Are they supporting the President?" Rather than looking to the White House for their directions, these men tended to keep their eyes turned toward the powerful Congressional committees.

Levine has portrayed the President as a man who is down-to-earth. He is puzzled, perplexed and quizzical as a result of the situation left to him by President Nixon's perfidy. T.B.

Lou Grant. "Another War Orphan". (1975). Ink, graphite and white paint on paper. 11⅝ × 9⅜". Collection the artist. Appeared in the *Oakland Tribune*, 1975.

*

No group of policy issues has proved more difficult for public officials to handle than those posed by the status of Vietnam. In the days following World War II, President Truman believed that the French could manage the Vietnamese problem if financing and arms were made available to them. President Eisenhower refused to go any further, and he would not permit the use of the U.S. Air Force to support the French. President Kennedy, on the other hand, provided both civilian and military aid. President Johnson—with wide support—dispatched a large portion of American conventional military power to Vietnam. Limited success persuaded him to begin negotiations for withdrawal, and President Nixon continued these negotiations with Henry Kissinger as his chief negotiator. It later became clear that the negotiated settlement was no settlement at all; and when large numbers of American troops were withdrawn, the remainder were pushed out of the country with their Vietnamese associates. The defeat in Vietnam exasperated both the American public and the Congress, with Kissinger bearing the brunt of the criticism.

To be sure, Kissinger had been a principal in the attempt to settle the problems by negotiation. But responsibility for failure was not limited to him; a long series of political, military and diplomatic mistakes had made his task almost insoluble. In the practical world, however, the last man to handle affairs gets blamed if the undertaking has been unsuccessful.

Lou Grant comments on Kissinger's position by placing him in the category of a war orphan. He displays a sensitivity to this position as he prophesied the future. Liberals and conservatives alike were arguing that Kissinger was responsible for the nation's international problems. He became a "war orphan" with few people willing to give him the consideration given to other war orphans.   T.B.

Note: A comprehensive bibliography dealing with cartoons, caricature, political art and the American Presidency would be out of place in a volume of this kind. The following suggestions may be useful for those who wish to read further. Each volume contains extensive bibliographic references.

Caricature and Cartoons

Becker, C. R., *Comic Art in America* (New York, 1959)

Gonbrich, E. H., and Kris, Ernst, *Caricature* (London, 1940)

Hess, Stephen and Kaplan, Milton, *The Ungentlemanly Art* (New York, 1968)

Hoffmann, Werner, *Caricature from Leonardo to Picasso* (New York, 1957)

Kunzle, David, *The Early Comic Strip* (Berkeley, 1973)

Larkin, Oliver, *Art and Life in America* (New York, 1964)

Murrell, William, *A History of American Graphic Humor* (New York, 1933)

Nevins, Allan and Weitenkampf, Frank, *A Century of Political Cartoons* (New York, 1944)

Stikes, Ralph, *The Indignant Eye* (Boston, 1964)

Weitenkampf, Frank, *American Graphic Art* (New York, 1912)

Weitenkampf, Frank, *Political Caricature in the United States* (New York, 1971)

The Presidency

Abramson, Henry J., *Justices and Presidents* (New York, 1975)

Binkely, Wilfred, *The Presidents and Congress* (New York, 1947)

Burns, James MacGregor, *Presidential Government* (Boston, 1973)

Butterfield, Roger, *The American Past* (New York, 1947)

Hofstadter, Richard, *The American Political Tradition* (New York, 1948; revised 1973)

Lorant, Stephan, *The Glorious Burden, The American Presidency* (New York, 1968)

Milton, George Fort, *The Use of Presidential Power, 1789-1943* (Boston, 1944)

Neustadt, Richard, *Presidential Power* (New York, 1960)

Rossiter, Clinton, *The American Presidency* (New York, 1960)

White, Theodore, *The Making of the President, 1960* (New York, 1961) [Successive volumes deal with the elections of 1964, 1968 and 1972; New York, 1965, 1969 and 1973]

Photographic Credits
Most photographs were provided by respective lenders
without specified credit; those specified photographers
are as follows:
Geoffrey Clements Photography, Staten Island, New
York: no. 86
Colin McRae, Berkeley: nos. 74, 79, 84, 87, 89, 90, 91,
93, 98, 106, 113
Library Photo Service, Berkeley: nos. 4, 24-28, 30-46, 48,
50-54, 56-62, 64, 66, 69, 75, 80, 85, 94, 99-104, 107-111

Typography is Palatino set by Allen Taplin, Oakland.
Offset lithograpy is by Cal Central Press, Sacramento.
Black and white reproductions are printed in 200 line
screen, single color. Color reproductions are printed
in 200 line screen, 4-color process. Cover paper is
Huskie c1s. Textpaper is 80 lb. Westland Opaque.
Color divider pages are 70 lb. Cardinal Groove.
Design is by Bruce Montgomery.